365 WAYS TO LIVE THE LAW OF ATTRACTION

HARNESS THE POWER OF POSITIVE THINKING EVERY DAY OF THE YEAR

MEERA LESTER

Avon, Massachusetts

Published by
Adams Media, a division of F+W Media, Inc.
57 Littlefield Street, Avon, MA 02322. U.S.A.
www.adamsmedia.com

Contains materials adapted and abridged from *The Everything® Law of Attraction Book*
by Meera Lester, copyright © 2008 by F+W Media, Inc.,
ISBN 13: 978-1-59869-775-9, ISBN 10: 1-59869-775-7.

ISBN 13: 978-1-4405-0050-3
ISBN 10: 1-4405-0050-9

Printed in the United States of America.

J I H G F E D C B A

Library of Congress Cataloging-in-Publication Data
is available from the publisher.

This publication is designed to provide accurate and authoritative information with
regard to the subject matter covered. It is sold with the understanding that the publisher
is not engaged in rendering legal, accounting, or other professional advice. If legal advice
or other expert assistance is required, the services of a competent professional person
should be sought.

> —From a *Declaration of Principles* jointly adopted by a Committee of the
> American Bar Association and a Committee of Publishers and Associations

Many of the designations used by manufacturers and sellers to distinguish their product
are claimed as trademarks. Where those designations appear in this book and Adams
Media was aware of a trademark claim, the designations have been printed with initial
capital letters.

This book is available at quantity discounts for bulk purchases.
For information, please call 1-800-289-0963.

Contents

Introduction

This book provides different lenses from a variety of disciplines through which you might view the concept of harmonious alignment with the Law of Attraction to draw into your life the things you desire. You may seek spiritual advancement and want to learn how the law is understood within various spiritual traditions. Perhaps you are more interested in how to achieve robust health or longevity. Maybe you desire to attract some of the finer things in life such as a sleek, new car, a lovely piece of jewelry, or a new set of china. Or, you hope to attract the perfect romantic partner, a well-paying job, path to a new career, or happiness and peace of mind.

Those are perfectly reasonable and attainable goals. But even if they weren't, it doesn't matter because whatever you most desire and think about most often is sure to manifest. You can have whatever you want. The universal Law of Attraction is always working to produce in your life the experiences, relationships, and things that you think about most. So if you are worried about breaking a bone, you will likely draw it in. Fear attracts more of the thing you fear. Here's another example. Your worry about an inability to meet your financial obligations results in bringing you more of the same. You are already drawing into your life both positive and negative experiences through the power of your thought.

But take heart. The good news is that the reverse is also true. When you desire to manifest money, your desire yoked with feelings of excited anticipation that money is coming from myriad sources, both known and unknown, can bring you financial prosperity. You can both not only shift your thoughts to bring more positive and happy experiences, but through transformational thinking, you can radically change your life. And it doesn't stop there. Aligned harmoniously with the Law of Attraction and with other like-minded people, you can work together to bring about change in the world. You and everyone who is deliberately working with the Law of Attraction become co-creators with the Divine through the power of your heart and mind.

There are certain basic steps to working with the law, but the approaches to those steps are necessarily as varied and unique as the person using them. You'll need to cultivate trust in the process, a feeling that you are worthy to receive the things you desire, openness to receive, an attitude of gratitude, and an understanding how to magnetize your desire thoughts with feeling and emotion.

These steps are not difficult steps to master. With the insights provided in this book you will soon be engaging in the transformational thinking that brings about exciting and positive life changes. How much or how little you want to shift the paradigm of your life and relationships depends upon you.

CHAPTER 1

Steps You Can Take . . .

to Change Your Perception

An Ancient Teaching with Many Names

1. An Ancient Teaching with Many Names

Modern spiritual seekers have called the Law of Attraction a recently discovered ancient secret teaching. Indeed, the law is ancient in its origins. Whether or not it was ever lost or purposefully kept secret could be argued, but what is true is that through the centuries, various spiritual teachers, philosophers, and others have mentioned or discussed the Law of Attraction, albeit calling it by various names in their teachings or writings. Today, renewed interest in the subject has catapulted the ages-old concept into mainstream popular culture while simultaneously placing it under a lens of scrutiny.

You may already be familiar with the concept of the law. The popular books and CDs about the Law of Attraction by Americans Esther and Jerry Hicks and Canadian Michael Losier, among others, as well as the mega hit, *The Secret*, by Australian Rhonda Byrne have put principles of that universal spiritual law into greater public awareness.

2. How the Law Works

If you've heard old adages such as, "like attracts like," "birds of a feather flock together," "as above, so below," and "what you send out comes back multiplied many times over," or the words in the New Testament spoken by Jesus, "ask and ye shall receive," then you may have an idea of what the Law of Attraction is. Simply put, the Law of Attraction asserts that a person's thoughts attract objects, people, and situations and circumstances, both positive and negative, into his or her life. Proponents of the Law of Attraction assert that the law brings you what you desire when you are 1) clear about what you want, 2) energize your desire for the item with thoughts, emotion, visual imagery and also talk about it and believe it is coming, and 3) feel and express gratitude for what you already have and that which you desire, even if it has not yet come into your experience.

3. Attraction Can Bring What You Do or Don't Want

Proponents of the Law of Attraction say that the law brings you whatever you think about most. Thoughts can become emotionally charged. When you desire something, say, a new outfit, you also feel emotion each time your mind thinks about having that new dress, jacket, shoes, and handbag. You are filled with excitement at the possibility of having your desire fulfilled. You believe you can have it. You deserve it. It is coming. You consider ways to speed up getting that outfit. You might even develop a plan of action for getting the money to go shopping at the mall.

4. Origins of the Law

According to some who have studied it, the universal great Law of Attraction has been with us since the beginning of time, perhaps even at the moment of creation and the beginning of thought. Others say it is impossible to pinpoint exactly when the concept entered human consciousness.

Some self-help experts say the Law of Attraction possibly dates as far back as 6,000 to 7,000 years ago where it found expression in the mystical traditions and beliefs of the ancients. Magicians of long ago certainly observed and wrote about affinities between things before the advent of science. Translations of ancient texts suggest that our spiritual ancestors thought a lot about the heaven and earth and all the creatures that existed as well as pondered the relationships between things.

5. The Law in Modern Times

Some say the Law of Attraction concept is possibly just an updated version of the teachings of the late Wallace Wattle (1860–1911) and those of Dr. Norman Vincent Peale (1898–1993). Wattle, who was born into poverty and became wealthy, wrote about the science of getting rich. Peale became famous for his ideas about the power of positive thinking. Both men emphasized the role of conscious and intensely focused thought in achieving the desired goal. Both men believed in a higher power at work in human lives. Wattles referred to it as "formless" intelligence and substance. Peale, a clergyman, spoke and wrote the power and presence of God.

6. Be Aware of Your Thoughts

It is important to understand that your thoughts can attract things you do not want. Whatever you fear most and think about often or obsessively can also manifest. For example, you may love hiking, but your greatest fear is that someday you'll encounter a rattlesnake. Repetitive thoughts that are charged with fear can set up the experience unless you let go of it. It is better to banish such dark thoughts. Don't give up hiking in the desert. Instead, be measured, thoughtful, studied, and prudent about undertaking such a hike. Know what precautions to take in order to have a safe hike. Replace your fearful thoughts with a sure-fire belief in a higher power working through you and with you at all times ensuring your safety.

7. Let Go of the Negatives, Focus on the Positives

A thorough understanding of the fundamentals of the Law of Attraction allows us to quickly achieve our goals and get more of the stuff we want and avoid attracting the things we do not want. With deliberate and focused application of the principles of the Law of Attraction, we can all achieve our full human potential and perhaps work together toward creating a more harmonious and just world.

The Law of Attraction, as already noted, works in response to thoughts that have become energized. What if you deliberately focused your attention on something that you wanted to call forth in your life . . . something you deeply desired to manifest? Would the Law of Attraction bring it to you? The answer is yes. Always.

8. Anyone Can Use It

Anyone can work with the Law of Attraction to deliberately make choices about what he wants and doesn't want in his life. He can use the law to help him work out his dreams, desires, and ambitions. So, too, he can repel the things he does not want. Indebtedness worries, for example, can bring more debt. But when thoughts of poverty are replaced by images of abundance, the Law of Attraction springs into action to replace lack with abundance.

The Law of Attraction is not wishful thinking, daydreaming, or momentary flights of fancy. A wish is not a strong enough intention. The law is always working to give people the very things they most desire.

9. Know that Anything is Possible

At first it may seem impossible that a person could shrink his debt, acquire wealth, and grow that wealth as much as his mind could imagine. But the Law of Attraction makes anything possible. There are myriad books, CDs, tapes, etc. to teach individuals how to get rich. Often such books offer advice about how to assess your indebtedness, develop a financial plan, imagine putting every step of the plan in place, visualize what's going to happen, and actualize the events. In this way, the person accelerates the working of the Law of Attraction.

Many people believe that divine consciousness permeates the universe and that when they align themselves in harmony with that consciousness, they become co-creators with the Divine of their destinies. Individuals can tap into the realm of infinite potential and substance. Through their thoughts, they draw into their lives all circumstances, situations, relationships, experiences, and things. The process is continuous and unending.

10. Your Imagination is a Powerful Tool

Whether dreaming or awake, the mind thinks in images and symbols. Proponents of the Law of Attraction say that when we can clearly imagine having what we most want, the Law of Attraction takes over and gives it to us.

The time it takes for a dream to become reality doesn't really matter so much as getting the desired result. Some experts on the Law of Attraction have pointed out that as soon as someone begins focusing on the thing he or she really wants, the universe gets busy arranging or rearranging the necessary elements and circumstances to make manifestation of that thing possible. The process can be accelerated with a little planning.

11. Put Your Mind to Work for You

A debt-free life, new friends, a loving life partner, plenty of money, a new car, or the dream job—whatever the person desires will manifest. When someone decides to accelerate the process and works out a plan to allow for that manifestation, myriad opportunities begin to present themselves. A person working with the Law of Attraction need only to change his or her mindset and be aware that the opportunities for manifestation of his or her desire will become more commonplace. It is as if the universe is working with you, putting wind in the sail of your dream ship to take you anywhere you want to go and give you the experiences, relationships, money, wealth, and things you most desire.

12. The Law Is Unbiased

The Law of Attraction does not judge the value or worth of your thoughts. It cares not whether they are harmful or well intentioned.

Nor does it value whether or not your thought arises from a particular belief system. You may eschew religion and be an atheist or agnostic. Or, you may be deeply religious. Knowledge and practice of a spiritual tradition (or lack of belief) doesn't concern the working of the law. What matters is how you feel about what you are thinking.

Gratitude plays a role because of how it makes you feel. For example, when you are grateful for having something, you feel good and the thoughts of "having" and the positive feelings of "having" bring more of the same. The law always responds to what you are focusing on in your thoughts and the emotion generated in response to those thoughts, since feeling strengthens the attracting power of thought.

13. Kindness Begets Kindness

Thinking good thoughts instead of dark or evil ones is a way of doing good. When you silently bless others, that is a good thing and good is attracted back into your life. You've no doubt heard the phrase, "what goes around comes around." It comes back to magnetic attraction. When you pray and do good deeds (acts of kindness like putting money in an expired parking meter where a stranger's car is parked), your thoughts and actions bear the fruit of goodness. Consider for a moment what kinds of thoughts and feelings, mental images, words, and deeds are you sending out? What is in your life that you don't like? What would you change? What do you desire?

14. **Deliberate Intention Takes Focus**

Think of how something looks under a magnifying glass or a microscope. The subject being studied comes into crisp focus and is magnified many times. This is what you do when you work with the Law of Attraction. With deliberate intention, your thoughts necessarily become not only highly focused but more concentrated and energized. You must have the intent of receiving what you wish for and not waver in your belief that the manifestation is already in the works. Dream what may have been for you the impossible dream before you knew about the Law of Attraction. Now you understand that anything you desire will be possible to achieve or have. The Law of Attraction is continually responding to whatever you are thinking and feeling.

15. **Clear Your Mind**

As previously stated, the Law of Attraction is unbiased. Whatever you think about is what is manifested. Careless thinking about negative events and people who just want to exploit others can just as easily draw similar negative experiences and individuals into your life. Most likely you'll protest and declare that you would never want those things to happen; you would never have deliberately drawn them to you. But when you begin to correlate your thinking with events that have happened or are occurring in your life, you will begin to see how your thoughts influence your life experiences.

If you think you are doing everything correctly to manifest your desires but they haven't come to you as yet, perhaps you need to clear some clutter and make a space for it, in other words, create a vacuum.

16. The Law Works When There Is a Vacuum

If someone wants to manifest something in his work or life experience, he or she may first have to create the space for it. In other words, tear down, remove, and otherwise clean and clear a space to make it ready to receive the object or create the right climate for getting a new job, raise in pay, loving companion, or new group of friends. The ancient Chinese tradition known as Feng Shui emphasizes the clearing of space and the art of placement to attract the things you desire to have in your life. Clutter impedes or blocks energy flow and when you are trying to bring something good into your life, you certainly don't want to block its arrival.

You can use the principles of Feng Shui to enhance your intentional work with the Law of Attraction, especially if you are seeking harmony, peace, and prosperity in all areas of life. One of the major maxims of Feng Shui states, "less is more."

17. Test the Law of Attraction for Yourself

When you open the space in your life to manifest something, the substance of the universe will fill it, according to Catherine Ponder, author of *The Dynamic Laws of Prosperity*. If you are experiencing lack when you seek abundance, look first to your thoughts. Are they positive? Have you unwittingly created any blockages? If so, remove them. Create a vacuum for what you want. Riches, expensive jewelry, a new house, a hot car, a super healthy body, a new husband or boyfriend, spiritual insights, weight loss, or even a business of your own—you can have whatever you want. That's the promise of the law when you work deliberately with it.

18. Dare to Join the Dance of Transformation

Like the Hindu god Shiva Nataraja, who dances the universe into creation and destruction, you can change your destiny by destroying patterns of negative thought and replacing them with positive thinking and feeling. Shiva's dance destroys ignorance and awakens the latent divine force of kundalini, the sacred energy that conveys mortal consciousness to a state of enlightenment. Through your powerful intentions and aligned with the Law of Attraction, perhaps you, too, will awaken from the dark slumber of unintentionally attracting what you don't want to, instead, drawing into your life what you do want. There is enormous power in every moment of every day to change your patterns of thinking, and thus, the potential future karmic ramifications of your thoughts, words, and deeds.

Steps You Can Take . . .

to Train Your Mind

19. Calm Your Restless Thoughts

To deliberately utilize the Law of Attraction, it's important to understand how the mind works and then train it as your tool. If you have practiced meditation, you've experienced the mind's restless nature. Thoughts keep jumping around because of word associations, direct linkage, or internal and external stimuli. Learn to train your mind to stay on topic. Contemplate all things related to the object or circumstance that you seek to manifest. Wrap your thoughts around your desire, sharpen your focus, and feel expectant to draw the desired object to you.

20. Matter and Energy

Atoms are the building blocks of matter while energy has been called the workhorse of creation. From grade-school science, you may have learned that the energy of the universe can change from one form to another, seem to disappear, move about, or remain available as potential energy. You probably also learned about the two main categories of energy—kinetic, or energy in motion, and potential, or energy that is stored or in position to be released. Both energy types have relevance to the Law of Attraction.

21. Your Thoughts Produce Energy

Energy is what enables the work of the entire universe to get done whether the work is fueling the tasks of creation or simply digesting food or thinking thoughts. When you eat a meal, your body receives the energy from the food it has digested. It stores excess calories to be accessed later.

Many practitioners of the Law of Attraction have noted that the interrelationship between thoughts and things is dependent on the psychic energy generated by creative thought. Such energized thought sets up the attraction. Just as the mind can use the power of creative and positive thought to attract things, such as healing in the body, it can also attract objects and situations it desires through thought energy.

22. Your Thoughts Are Things

Some people believe that our lives express our interior worlds, or what we think about. You have undoubtedly heard the saying that "thoughts are things." In fact, in Hinduism, nothing exists apart from the Divine because it permeates all things.

Certain psychics, mediums, and empathic people possess a heightened sense of the electromagnetic energy that is retained in objects, haunted houses, sacred places, crime scenes, and the like. Psychic energy lives on in those objects and places.

Even as doctors work in integrative medicine (using both western and eastern medical knowledge) and high performance sports experts counsel their athletes about an intrinsic mind/body connection, scientific research continues on the subject of thoughts as energy.

23. Thoughts Can Be Felt

Energy of one type can change or be converted into a different type. Although invisible to the naked eye, energy may be perceived and felt. It's been said that "you can't fool kids or dogs" because they have a natural ability to sense whether someone's energy and intention toward them is good or bad. Kids and dogs may be able to detect more readily than others the feelings or mood of another that is being generated by thought.

24. Shakti: Psychic Energy Lingers

In India, modern spiritual seekers make pilgrimages to the sacred places associated with holy ones of the past because the Shakti (divine energy or holy psychic energy) of those beings remains in the places where those saints had prayed, meditated, and became enlightened. Many modern spiritual seekers further believe that the energy stored in the sacred places energetically charged by the holy ones of the past has a beneficial effect on their spiritual efforts to attain enlightenment. Contact with the shakti of enlightened beings, although those saints no longer live in human form, could awaken the Kundalini Shakti, the innate and essential divine energy that leads human consciousness to union with God (or Absolute divine consciousness) as the energy makes its ascent from the base of the spine to the energy center located on top of the head. The modern seekers' thought, magnetized by their spiritual desire for enlightenment, could manifest their desire (making their thought become the thing they most ardently seek and desire).

25. Prana: The Life Force is Everywhere

Pranic energy represents a kind of bridge between thoughts becoming or manifesting as things. In ancient Hindu writings, the body's vital airs or energies were referred to as prana. Pranic energy permeates all things, including the human mind (and, thus, thought), according to the Hindu sacred scriptures known as the Upanishads. Those sacred writings associated prana, which means "breath" in Sanskrit, with vitality and expressed the idea that a person's prana survives throughout eternity or until a being's soul once again reincarnates. Prana, often mistakenly thought of as breath, is more correctly understood as a life-sustaining force. Prana underlies and sustains the universe, according to Hindu belief. Prana, therefore, is found in thoughts and also material objects. The pranic energy of one human, for example, directed toward another person or object can trigger a response, reaction, or change. Even an energized or magnetized thought can instantly or eventually become the thing that the psychic energy of the creative mind conceives, giving rise to the New Age idea that "thoughts are things."

26. Chi: Harmony and Balance

The Chinese use the word "chi" (pronounced *chee*) to mean the natural, supernatural, and spiritual energy of the physical universe and the human body and mind. An imbalance of chi in a person's body or life brings upon him or her disharmony and disease. Practitioners of acupuncture, chi gong, and other disciplines embracing the concept of chi as a subtle force underlying and permeating all things (like prana) say that restoring the balance of the flow of the chi is what restores balance, health, and harmony. When balance is restored, the things a person desires become manifest through their thought energy.

27. Subtle Energies Influence Healing

Aura healing, chakra healing, reiki (pronounced RAY kee), quantum touch, and no-touch healing are all examples of alternative medicine/belief systems that suggest the vital energy of the body, whether called prana, chi, ki, or life force, can be manipulated. Skeptics classify such healings as faith-healing and say if it works at all it is because of the thoughts of the patient—the placebo effect—that is, the patient believes something is being done to help him feel better, he hopes he will, and subsequently he does. Some might say that the placebo effect causes changes in the patient's neurochemistry (due to his positive thinking that he would be healed) that might, in part, explain the healing he subsequently received.

28. The Polarity of Thought Energy

Your thought energy flows either inward or outward. If it is stationary, meaning not flowing in either direction, then it lacks any energy to carry your intention inward or outward. Intention, or your desire for something, requires energy and polarity to manifest that desire. If you need healing from a chronic illness or seek spiritual unfolding, you will focus your thought energy or polarity inward, whereas, if you desire a new house or car, you'll focus the polarity outward. Another way to think of it is that when the energy is polarized outward, you become engaged in some action—you create or do something. When the polarity is turned inward, you acquire or become the recipient of something.

Some Law of Attraction teachers have explained the outward and inward polarities of thought energy as follows: outward polarity requires an action of giving something to the universe; inward polarity requires a receptive state in which you receive something from the universe. Understanding the concept is vital to putting the Law of Attraction into work in a deliberate way in your life.

29. Turning Your Thoughts Outward

If you have the desire and intention to launch a business, write a screenplay, or build a bridge, invent a better mousetrap, or establish a women's collective in a Third World country, your thoughts have an outward polarity. The thing you hope to manifest is not so much for you as it is an outward expression of something you wish to do or accomplish. Other examples of outward polarity might include creating a beautiful concrete statue and covering it with mosaics for your local community park, establishing an oral history program that links children with senior citizens in your town, starting a new business or nonprofit venture, or even writing a novel or screenplay. Think of these manifestations as your gift to the universe.

30. The Power to Attract and Repel

Have you ever met people who were so self-focused that they seemed to derive pleasure from dwelling on all the things that were going wrong in their life? They couldn't seem to quit talking about their woes. Perhaps you wondered what was wrong with that person that his or her life was so out of control and beset with one crisis after another and enough problems to last several lifetimes. Their outer life may simply be a reflection of their interior world. Knowingly or unwittingly, that person is attracting more of what he or she is thinking about most. And most likely, he or she is dwelling on everything that could go wrong or get worse.

31. Accentuate the Positive

Our thoughts can lift us to joyful heights or cause us to sink in the depths of despair. When we are thinking positively, we bring or attract positive situations and people. But when we are focused on the negative aspects of our life, we attract more negativity. Our thoughts are often charged with positive or negative emotion and are rarely neutral.

If you want more goodness in your life, be good and be grateful. Feel joy and peace and happiness. Spread it out into the universe as your gift to others. Keep your mind clean from clutter, worry, and fear. Don't give mental energy to negative thinking. Just let it go. Focus on the positive to draw more of that into your life.

32. Like Attracts Like

That sums up how the Law of Attraction works. It is not possible for the law to be biased. If you are a happy, upbeat person with a smile for everyone, expect to find friends and good experiences wherever you go. Your thoughts bring those experiences into your life. On the other hand, if you are more like a curmudgeon, with a negative attitude, a sour expression, and complaints about everything (including each ache and pain in your body), do not be surprised if people avoid you and disease, disaster, and disappointment seem to lurk around every corner.

33. Follow the Six Basic Steps of Manifesting

An understanding of the fundamentals of the Law of Attraction is the foundation upon which to build your house of dreams. To get started with the work of bringing into your life experience the various circumstances and things that you desire, read and follow the following list of steps. Each is simple and easy to do whenever you have a quiet moment during the day.

1. Clear the clutter, confusion, and negativity from your mind.
2. Set forth the intention to manifest something. Make a mental declaration of your intent.
3. Be expectant. Be ready to receive. Believe you deserve it, and it is already yours.
4. Visualize yourself having it.

5. Feel and express gratitude for the blessings you already have, the gifts of the universe that the higher power makes available to you, and for the power that makes possible each manifestation.

6. Repeat these steps often each day.

34. Think of the Six Steps as Exercise

You can ramp up the energy of your thought, turning it into a high-energy idea or concept, just as you can build muscle in your body. It just takes practice and frequent repetition of the six basic steps. There are many other things you can do as well to intensify the energy about your intention.

Even if you skip a day or two of focused thinking about your intention to manifest your desire, your desire is still there. Over time the thought energy around your intention may weaken, but if the desire is still strong, the object, situation, or relationship can still come into your life experience but simply may take longer to manifest.

35. Use Symbolism to Focus Your Intention

In Jungian psychology, symbolism has always served as an important and powerful tool, especially in the healing process. Patients are often encouraged to focus on symbols that embody special meaning for them. These symbols may appear in a patient's dreams or in their mindless scribbles and doodles. Those symbols deemed most potent may become departure points or pathways inward into the psyche.

Use a specific symbol that holds cultural or spiritual meaning for you. Use the symbol throughout the day and also at bedtime as a reminder to meditate or visualize having the thing most desired. Place the image on a refrigerator, bathroom mirror, or bedside table where it can be easily seen.

36. The Universal Power of Symbols

There are literally thousands of symbols, from ancient to modern. Some may have obscure meanings while others are universally understood. While certain symbols may be associated with myths and cultural traditions, others hold special meaning only for certain groups.

Some symbols have represented a specific meaning for centuries. Symbols such as a wheel, rose, key, cross, and a lotus still represent a mystical entry into transcendental states of consciousness and hidden knowledge or wisdom. However, such symbols may also have other meanings associated with them, depending upon the culture in which they are found. For example, the cross, a sacred symbol for Christians, is also the symbol of earth to the Chinese.

37. Symbols Can Represent Transcendental Consciousness

Symbols have the power to alter consciousness if they are used for such purpose. For example, perhaps you desire to use a symbol to represent a metaphysical truth or a transcendent state of mind. Consider the Hindu symbol for AUM as a point of reflection. It is believed to be the sound of the cosmic vibration of the universe. The yin/yang symbol that represents the opposite principles of masculine and feminine in Chinese philosophy means for some people harmony, balance, and universal fellowship. A dragon or bear image suggests strength and fortitude.

38. Find a Potent Symbol with Personal Meaning

Perhaps there is some object that has deep personal meaning for you that you wanted long ago and still do not have. Perhaps there is a certain symbol that always reminds you of that object. If, one day, you find yourself cutting out a magazine picture, and discover that it's of a lipstick red, Porsche convertible, just know your subconscious still wants that car. Go for it. The magazine picture will be a good reminder for you to work with the Law of Attraction to manifest it.

39. Look to Your Dreams for Symbols

The same is true if you have a recurring dream about, say, searching for a key while traversing the top of a mountain. Such a dream might be pointing to a search for the wisdom key and higher states of consciousness as represented by the mountain. It could also mean the challenges you have faced reaching the top (success in achieving your goals, etc.).

You may find a powerful symbol in the dreamtime to use as a touchstone for your work of consciously manifesting. Working with your dreams can be fun, intriguing, and instructive.

Steps You Can Take . . .

to Activate Your Power

40. Love is Essential

Humans require love to flourish. Love energizes thoughts, empowers individuals to dream and follow their bliss, and enables their efforts to manifest. In his best-selling book, *Think and Grow Rich*, author Napoleon Hill explained that it is by our predominate thoughts that we thrive. Many people might agree that when thoughts are of love, they leave a deep "imprint" in our psyches and hearts. We become powerful creators when we learn to transmute negative thoughts into positive ones, for example, anger into appreciation, and then magnetize our thoughts with love.

41. Love is a Magnetizer

Love can serve as a powerful magnetizer for manifesting. Here's the way it works. Because of the hormones that are released in your body when you are in love, your thoughts become highly magnetized. When you first fall in love, you may feel crazy and even somewhat obsessive. All you can think about is your beloved. The other person may, in fact, be thinking of you in the exact moment that you are thinking of him or her.

Whether altruistic, romantic, or compassionate, love seeks expression. Passionate love is the driving force behind magnificent works of art, architecture, literature, and music as well as procreation. Many of us became the expression of our parents' love for each other. Love can draw into your life a romantic partner, meaningful work, pets, and friends.

42. Love Promotes Creativity

Some artists, who have not yet experienced success, may feel a love for their craft but do not have the optimism, confidence, and sense of expectancy that they can create something unique and exceptional. Perhaps their love for their craft is not as strong as their sense of defeatism or failure, which can sabotage their efforts. And yet, others use their pain and suffering as images in their work. Love pulls them into their work and passion serves as the catalyst that ignites their vision for what they desire to manifest. Such artists may become highly successful, turning out magnificent and unique works as their gifts to the world.

43. Get Close to the Source

When you calm your mind, cultivate a positive mood, center your thoughts on the outcome your desire, and love what you are doing, you are in a position to optimally manifest that which your heart most desires. Wallace Wattles, writing is his 1910 book *The Science of Getting Rich*, noted that when you live closer to the source of wealth and abundance and align yourself in harmony with that, you get more of what you seek from the source. Living closer to the source, as Wattles calls it, might suggest to some readers to think of that unnamed, unknowable source of all with appreciation, gratitude, and love. Such emotionally charged thought attracts more of the same to the individual.

44. A Response for Skeptics

While some critics shrilly denounce the Law of Attraction as being pure bunk, others temper their remarks with a reminder that positive thinking and instilling hope is a good thing. If believing in the Law of Attraction inspires one to have a better life, set some goals, and reach for treasured dreams, so much the better. French-born diarist Anais Nin once remarked that a life shrinks or expands according to one's courage. Sometimes it takes courage to just believe in something and allow for its unfolding in your life.

45. Start with the Energy of Manifestation

For manifestation to take place, energy must be expended. The process begins with a desire to have something, let's say, a new friend who will become your romantic partner and possibly your future husband. In a measured and thoughtful manner, you think about what you want as clearly as you can. Next, your imagination wraps around new qualities, traits, or skills that you hope he will have. The more you think about exactly what you want, the more refined the image of your new mate becomes—he can cook, dance the salsa, and romp with the kids and dog with a wild spontaneity. Imaginative thoughts of interacting with such a person gives you pleasure and your thoughts of him become charged with positive emotion.

46. Put Yourself Out There

Up to this point, you have been using energy in your thinking, imagining, visualizing, and making lists. Now you decide to put yourself into situations where you might actually meet him. You attend a speed-dating event with a friend, sign up for a month on an Internet matchmaking site, frequent bookshops and grocery stores, and take a cooking class. You start taking your dog on extended walks, believing that at any moment he may soon walk toward you. You tell your friends and family members you are ready for him to show up and believe he's near.

47. Let the Seed Grow

Using mental, emotional, and physical energy, you have sown the seed of desire. The task of a seed sown in fertile ground is to sprout and grow. Let the universe do the work. It takes time for a seed to germinate and push up so you can actually see it growing. Even though you cannot see the germination and growth process, you must nourish it and have faith that it will spring forth in fullness.

48. You Will Soon See the Result

According to the Law of Attraction experts, your expectation and anticipation will now pull the mate you seek into your life. Just as a mustard seed, at first appears so tiny and seemingly inconsequential, once sown in nourishing soil, can spring forth to become the greatest herb in the garden, so, too, will the dream in your heart sprout in its fullness. In the New Testament, Jesus explained in the Parable of the Sower the unseen power of the tiny mustard seed to grow into something great.

49. Enter the Realm of Infinite Possibility

Most of us have a materialistic side and go crazy when we see must-have items in our favorite catalogs or in the windows of neighborhood stores. We live in a credit card society where plastic can buy nearly every tangible thing known to humankind. Still, most of us hold off buying big-ticket items like houses and cars until we can afford them. That may mean waiting years, in some cases. But what if we set aside factors such as cost for a moment and considered the possibility of having anything our hearts desired? What if we didn't have to figure out how to get it and left that up to the universe to arrange? What if our job was simply to go shopping in the storehouse of the universe and reveal to the Source our desires? What if it were that simple? The Law of Attraction experts say it is.

50. Imagine the Source as Infinite Abundance

The great sages and saints of all religions learned to rely on the Unseen Power at work in the universe. That power provided them not only with wisdom and, in some case, enlightenment, but also took care of the food, clothing, and shelter needs of their human bodies.

In India, today, yogis or *rishis* still make pilgrimages to the forested mountains of Rishikesh in order to meditate undisturbed in natural settings of caves or under trees or near water. They depend upon the Unseen Power of the universe to take care of them while they perform their sadhana (tasks associated with devotion to a deity), undertake anusthans (spiritual practices to achieve a specific result), or spend untold hours in meditation, contemplation, and the recitation of chants.

51. It is Possible to Access Streams of Divine Power

According to the teachings of Hinduism, five streams of energy emanate from the cosmic Aum. While Aum itself is considered a manifestation of God, omnipresent in the form of *Shabda Brahma*, three of its five energy streams are known as Brahma (Creator), Vishnu (Sustainer), and Shiva (Destroyer). Yogis understand how to tap into the streams of Divine Power to achieve certain objectives.

The Gayatri Mantra, perhaps the most sacred of all mantras and considered the primordial mantra by Hindus, was projected into manifestation by the will of God in order to bring about the current cycle of creation, say Hindu religious scholars. The Divine energy known as Brahma then manifested all animate and inanimate objects in the universe.

52. Beings of Light and Truth Appear when They Are Needed

According to Hindu thought, all of creation expands and contracts in cycles. Certain cycles are characterized by lightness and darkness. When darkness is upon the earth, holy beings such as the Buddha, Mohammed, and Jesus appear on Earth as light bearers to lead humankind out of darkness, depravity, and despair back to light and truth. Some people believe that great and holy beings are always present and anonymously working to manifest good for the well-being of all.

53. Look to the Buddha's Example

The Buddha, a holy being who lived approximately five hundred years before Jesus, was the son of King Suddhodana, ruler of the Shakya people, in ancient India. One day he left the royal palace and first witnessed human suffering when he met an old man whose life and health were waning, an invalid, and a begging ascetic.

Desiring to find a way to defeat suffering, poverty, and infirmity, Siddhartha renounced his life, left his wife and son, and became an ascetic. Through meditation and the breathing technique of observing the in/out breaths (*anapana-sati*), he discovered the Middle Way, a spiritual path without extreme asceticism or sensual indulgences. He had followed his desire to its end. By achieving enlightenment, he defeated suffering, poverty, and infirmity.

54. The Source is Always Open

The Source of all things is available twenty-four hours a day, seven days a week. To work with the Law of Attraction is to trust that we can go to that divine Source for anything desired at any moment. Consider the possibility that we are to live in abundance, in good health, and surrounded by love. What is keeping us from living the kind of life we only dream of having? Perhaps nothing more than our own negative self-talk. If we don't believe we deserve the good things in life, the Law of Attraction won't bestow good things upon us.

55. Replace Negative Self-Talk

The twelve-step programs that are often key to the recovery of substance abusers advocate that people must take responsibility for their actions but that they can find help anytime by trusting in a higher power. Those who suffer addictions must learn to let go of negative self-talk as it defeats the good they are trying to manifest in their lives. Self-talk is the perpetual driver of behavior. It tells half-truths and untruths. Replacing negative self-talk with the statement reworded into a positive affirmation can literally change a life.

56. Seek Out Joy

Joy, according to several dictionary definitions, is the emotion of happiness or delight. It is triggered by the expectation of something good or satisfying. Joy, it has been said, is at the core of our being. A peaceful joyful countenance reflects a corresponding inner life. Seek joy for yourself and others and give the gift of silent blessing to all (especially those experiencing lack in their lives) that they will experience joy and success in every aspect of their lives.

57. Patience is a Virtue

Sometimes when you really want something specific in your life, the waiting can trigger frustration and doubt that it is ever coming. Those times are periods when you must learn to trust that the universe is doing its work. Your desire is known. Your intent has been proclaimed. Part of working with the Law of Attraction is letting go of the need to control the timeframe during which your desire manifests in your life. You have the capacity to let go of that compulsion and as the noted psychologist Carl Rogers once observed, "You can't push the river."

58. The Law of Attraction Works with Momentum

Things can manifest instantly or take a long time. Why? The reason has a lot to do with the strength of your desire, the clarity of your vision, and the power of your intention. Remember that the universe is rearranging itself to bring you what you want but it also allows for you to wrangle with your choice and all the different aspects, elements, and options your mind conceives.

Napoleon Hill, author of *Think and Grow Rich*, warned that indecision and doubt work together to become fear. The process or blending of the two, though steady and insidious, may not be obvious to the conscious mind. The end result is fear. But fear is a state of mind that can be altered by conscious thought.

Steps You Can Take . . .

to Respond to Critics

59. Blaming the Victim?

If you break your leg, did you attract that into your life? A plethora of books and DVD's such as *The Secret* by Australian author Rhonda Byrne, which was featured twice on Oprah, have ignited a national discussion about the Law of Attraction and the simple premise that you are attracting everything into your life through your thought. Yet some scientists and critics disagree with that concept. They say it blames the patient to suggest that he or she attracted the heart disease, death of a child, or plane crash.

60. Can it be Proven?

At best, detractors say, the Law of Attraction overstates a promise that just thinking about something brings it to you. Further, critics argue, irrefutable proof that you can gain whatever you dream about or long for, is not a tenable hypothesis that can be proven through scientific method. Instead, they point out, savvy marketing, attention-grabbing buzz words and catchy phrases along with the promise of getting something for (almost) nothing seems to have caught the imagination of Americans and the media.

61. Taking Advantage of Easy Targets?

The disenfranchised, poor, aged, infirmed, and gullible, critics say, have always been targets for schemes that make their lives easier. When thoughts about $100,000 and a Bentley or a miracle cure don't materialize, disappointment doesn't begin to describe the feelings of the person who had believed in the promise of the Law of Attraction.

Yet believers of the law have faith that it is always working to bring into your life the fruits of your thinking.

It's unlikely that you would attract into your life the parallel of an isolated thought about something frightening. However, the more you experience the fear and allow it build around a specific idea or image, the more likely you are to attract it.

62. Not a New Concept

As mentioned in the previous chapters, the concept of the Law of Attraction has resonance with older books containing similar ideas. *Think and Grow Rich* and *The Law of Success,* by Napoleon Hill; *The Science of Getting Rich,* by Wallace Wattles; *The Power of Positive Thinking,* by Norman Vincent Peale; and *How to Win Friends and Influence People,* by Dale Carnegie, are just a few titles from other eras that preceded the current offerings of Law of Attraction. The new works often feature a personal growth, self-help, or New Age focus while the aforementioned books targeted a different type of audience with content that was practical and inspirational.

63. Andrew Carnegie Knew the Secret

Napoleon Hill interviewed five hundred of the wealthiest men of his lifetime. Born into a poor Virginian family in 1883 and orphaned by the age of twelve, Hill overcame poverty to become a journalist and lawyer. Scotsman and steel titan Andrew Carnegie became his mentor. Carnegie felt that others, if they understood his formula for building a stupendous fortune, could likewise create wealth. He urged Hill to interview successful American businessmen like him to find out their success secrets. Hill did and subsequently shared his findings in books, lectures, and speeches.

64. Napoleon Hill's Formula for Success

Hill learned that any formula for wealth and success had to include such things as formulating a precise purpose, cultivating the desire for it to manifest, recognizing opportunity whenever and wherever it showed up, being persistent (don't give up too soon or take no for an answer), cultivating success consciousness (rather than failure thoughts), perceiving advantage and new opportunities in every obstacle and adversity, and perhaps most importantly, having a desire that is fueled by faith and charged with emotion. He also believed it wise to surround oneself with like-minded persons.

65. What Hill's Detractors Said

In his books, Hill wrote about his belief in the power of autosuggestion as a law of nature and suggested that our thoughts are like vibrations in the ether that are either negatively or positively charged by our emotions. The subconscious mind, according to Hill, must be influenced by emotionally charged thought mixed with faith if such thought is to bear results. Detractors believed that Hill's thinking was flawed. They asserted that it was foolhardy to believe desire could turn into its tangible equivalent. Further, they argued that it is impossible to create something out of nothing.

66. Infinite Potential is Available for All

Detractors say that the potential to acquire money and material things exists for a few but not everyone. Money is to be made by those who know how to capitalize on the Law of Attraction topic. The Law of Attraction teachers and coaches say that the law is always working and once you know how to work deliberately with it, you can draw whatever you want from the storehouse of the universe. You have the potential to manifest one dollar or a million dollars. You could establish a hospital, fund an orphanage, or build a social club for senior citizens. Anything you want to create is possible provided you have desire, intention, and persistence. You already have the means—your thoughts—assert proponents of the law. Your potential for manifesting is limitless.

67. Desire is the Key

Proponents of the Law of Attraction argue that people can create their lives on purpose. In every age and era, there are those who form a strong desire to do something important or meaningful with their lives. In some cases, the desire is simply to build a better mousetrap. In others, it's to give something back to the universe or to do something for the greater social good. Those individuals believe so strongly in what they want that they think about it all the time, perhaps even praying about it and seeking help from the highest Source.

68. Positive Thoughts Have Healing Power

Believers in the Law of Attraction argue that miracle cures, which doctors and science cannot explain, do, in fact, occur. They assert that it is nothing short of arrogant for us to believe that we humans know everything and that the power of healing isn't possible without our intervention with drugs and medical treatments. People in dire situations such as facing battle with a terminal disease often feel helpless and want to do something. Encouraging them to have positive thoughts and focus on the best-case scenario certainly offers a better option than dwelling on the worst-case scenario.

69. Outer Reality Mirrors What is Within

The Law of Attraction, according to its proponents, mirrors your interior world, manifesting in your life experience your thoughts because the law is always working whether you are conscious of it or not. This idea, argue the law's critics, suggests that a person who has been a victim of adverse circumstances has brought calamity upon herself. Whether she fell prey to identity theft, was laid off or recently fired from her job, involved in a car crash, bitten by a poisonous snake or attacked by a bobcat while running on a woodland trail, she became a victim. Critics assert that Law of Attraction believers fault the individual for such misfortunes. How, skeptics ask, does an unsuspecting, perhaps vulnerable person draw upon herself such calamity?

70. Lessons from Buddhism

Buddhism teaches that suffering arises when people are attached to their desires. In Buddhism, whether good or bad happens, it is not God or the Creator causing those things but karma. Every thought, word, and act has a consequence, according to Buddhists. A person must let go of attachment, be still and observant, and discover what is real and what is not.

Some say that the way to happiness and harmony is to simply observe whatever thoughts arise, whatever circumstances and situations life brings to you, and whatever happens, whether good or bad, avoid all reaction and attachment. In other words, be a witness to life's joys and agonies, without responding, reacting, or getting entangled. This way to peace has resonance in Buddhism.

71. Ask Critics to Consider the Possibilities

Just as the Law of Attraction ideas began to gain widespread attention, critics emerged from various corridors to voice concerns and divergent points of view. Those believing in the power of the universal law found themselves defending their belief in the powerful working of the law. They advised those who doubted to at least try to set aside their opposition and be open to the possibility that the law could work wonders in their lives. Their basic premise, they would tell skeptics, was that if positive thinking and a grateful attitude attracts the things you want, then the flip side of that idea is that negative thinking will draw to you the things you don't want.

72. **Only a Matter of Perception?**

Some critics say that the Law of Attraction is a nothing more than oversimplification of the Hindu and Buddhist idea of detachment or viewing life with equanimity, or an even mindedness. Hindu and Buddhist philosophies teach detachment and the avoidance of judging experiences as either good or bad so as not to be impacted by them; however, the Law of Attraction practitioners assert that it is, in fact, your thoughts that draw life experiences to you. You are not altering your relationship to or perception of an event. Instead, you are making it possible for it to take place through your emotions and thoughts.

73. **Many Renowned Figures Taught the Law**

Even as critics' voices have been rising to confront the basic tenets of the Law of Attraction and verbalize concerns for blaming victims (for attracting disease and negative experiences through their thoughts), producer Byrne and teachers of the law assert that many historical figures, specifically, Buddha, Hermes Trismegistus, Plato, Aristotle, Beethoven, and Isaac Newton knew about the law and secretly taught it. They say other teachers included Winston Churchill, Thomas Edison, Carl Jung, Albert Einstein, and Andrew Carnegie. More recent "teachers" included mythologist Joseph Campbell and civil rights leader Martin Luther King, whose perhaps most famous speech was built around the positive statement, "I have a dream."

74. Saints Perform Miracles

Critics say that some Law of Attraction teachers are ridiculous to suggest that creative imagination, visualizations, affirmations, and the power of positive thinking can help a person to manifest circumstances, objects, or healings. However, practitioners of the Law of Attraction point out that miraculous healings, even from seemingly incurable diseases, can and do happen. In the traditions of the Roman Catholic Church, before a person can continue to sainthood, three miracles have to have happened and be verified by the church as having no other explanation than intervention by the deceased holy person in response to prayer and faith of the petitioner.

75. By Any Other Name?

Wallace D. Wattles observed in his book, *The Science of Getting Rich*, that you shouldn't waste time daydreaming or building castles in the air but rather stick to a vision of yourself and your purpose with all the strength of the mind you are capable of mustering. There will always be those who believe in the power of positive thinking, whether or not they call it the Law of Attraction or by another name. Critics will also likely continue to weigh in on whether or not the Law of Attraction is actually a force at work in the lives of humans. It will be up to the individual to decide to believe the critics or the advocates of the law.

CHAPTER 5

Steps You Can Take . . .

to Expand Your Knowledge

76. Ancient Traditions and the Law of Attraction

Some people working with the Law of Attraction assert that any deliberate and concerted effort at manifesting involves nothing less than a new alchemy of transforming thought into physical matter. Further, they say the use of ancient wisdom practices can clarify and intensify efforts of deliberate manifesting in alignment with the Law of Attraction. Such practices draw upon traditions borrowed from the ancient Babylonians, Greco-Romans, Egyptians, Aborigines, Asians, and Aztecs and include working with dreams, studying mythological archetypes, and even magic.

77. Babylonians Used the Law of Attraction

A Babylonian named Hammurabi (1792–1750 B.C.) deeply desired to unify the scattered cities of Babylon into some kind of cohesive empire. He formulated a group of laws that came to be known as the Hammurabi Code. The Code contains two hundred and eighty-two laws that were forerunners to modern tort law. Hammurabi's system was fair and clearly articulated and most importantly, made possible the manifestation of his deepest desire, the unification of Babylonia. With his dream actualized, Hammurabi led the ancient Babylonians into a positive and productive period that scholars refer to as Babylon's golden age. Some Law of Attraction teachers say the ancient Babylonians understood the law, and their collective consciousness set up positive vibrations for good things to come to them.

78. Fear Attracts a Dark Destiny

According to the Old Testament book of Daniel, Nebuchadnezzar was a Babylonian king with dreams featuring negative images that only a young Israelite captive named Daniel could correctly interpret. Just as the Law of Attraction enabled Hammurabi to achieve his dream of a great and unified empire, it could also have brought about the decline of Nebuchadnezzar's empire because the law is always responding to positive and negative vibrations of a person's magnetized thoughts. Perhaps Nebuchadnezzar worried about a power shift taking place and Daniel's interpretations, as clear and seemingly irrefutable as they were, surely struck fear in the heart of the ruler.

79. Dreams and the Fall of Babylon

Daniel had predicted the fall of Babylon and the breaking up of the mighty empire into smaller and weaker kingdoms. Nebuchadnezzar's worst fears manifested within seventy years as the Persians invaded Babylon. Persia then fell into the hands of the Greeks led by Alexander the Great. Some might say that the Law of Attraction was simply bringing to Nebuchadnezzar what his fears and nightly dreams had attracted. Dreams can be incubated to elucidate some problem you may be encountering in a deliberate manifestation effort or to ensure that you are on course to achieve a goal. Likewise, dreams have been known to reveal illness, foretell births and deaths, and reveal breakthroughs in self-help and spiritual work.

80. Faith and Trust Bear the Fruits of Providence

There are many stories in the Old Testament about the desire, intent, dreams, faith, and will of the ancient Israelites to lay out a course for their destiny as children of the Lord. The Israelites believed that Moses had been chosen by God to lead them from their enslavement by Pharaoh to land that the Lord had promised them. Strong and steady characterizes their belief and faith that their dream of having their own special place in the world was sanctioned by the Lord. They also believed they were the Lord's chosen ones and that He remained ever near them. Their attitude that God would not abandon them kept their faith strong and that, in turn, kept fear and doubt in abeyance.

81. Collective Desire Creates Positive Results

When a leader and a group of people are holding a common vision for a goal, feeling expectant and joyful about the possibility of achieving it, and remaining focused while also putting energy toward accomplishing the goal every day, they are following a powerful recipe for success in manifesting their collective desire.

The Jews' goal was to get to the Promised Land even though it meant that they had to walk for forty years in the desert. Nevertheless, their belief that God was guiding them remained strong, steady, and focused. It allowed for their miraculous crossing of the Red Sea, safe passage through lands owned by their enemies, and, finally, entry to the Promised Land, the culmination of their jointly held dream.

82. How Alexander Became Great

In a discussion of the Law of Attraction, two words of Greek origin stand out: *eudaimonia*, meaning "human excellence and flourishing," and *anasa*, meaning "new beginnings." In ancient Greek history, a man named Alexander the Great epitomized the use of focused intention for beginning a new goal and a strong belief in one's personal excellence to manifest great things.

Before he died, Alexander managed to conquer the vast majority of the ancient world that was known to the Greeks of that time. He remained undefeated in battle. He clearly knew what goal he wanted to manifest in life and through the power of his thoughts, the intensity of his desire, and the Law of Attraction working with his thoughts and feelings, he became a formidable foe against his enemies.

83. A Dream Unites a Divided Egypt

One leader of the ancient world, King Narmar of Egypt, desired to unite Upper Egypt with Lower Egypt and lived to see his desire manifested. King Narmar's unification of Egypt had a profound and positive impact on all aspects of Egyptian life. His prosperity was revealed in a mace head discovered by archeologists. It showed the king with his bodyguards and provided a list of all his assets. His people likewise experienced a glorious period as a unified Egypt saw the building of pyramids and the development of hieroglyphics, more stability, and expanded trade. Some might say that those achievements stand as a powerful testament to the positive thinking and the hopes, dreams, and deeds of the Egyptian people and their visionary leader.

84. Self Mastery Can Achieve Spiritual Results

Rosicrucians believe that the key to gaining the mastery of life lies in your personal power and the source for all power is found within. With such mastery, you attain also strength, peace, and wisdom. The Law of Attraction works to help you achieve that mastery when you are attuned to the source. Harmoniously in tune with the universal spiritual laws, such as the Law of Attraction, you draw to you that which you need to further your spiritual unfolding.

To study the Rosicrucian way requires that a person seeks truth, has an open mind, a positive mental outlook, and clear aspirations for spiritual understanding. In other words, positive thinking and clarity of life goals can greatly impact the results you seek.

85. Manifest Your Highest Potential

The Rosicrucians teach that spiritual seekers in their organization will learn about the workings of the natural laws over all realms as well as discover the interconnectedness of all metaphysical teachings and also increase understanding of self.

For those seeking better health, abundant career opportunities, better family relationships, or stepped-up personal growth, the Rosicrucian Order and other spiritual traditions can reveal how to actualize those desires. People can literally re-set a new course for their lives once they understand the wisdom ways taught by the Rosicrucian Order. The path believers walk is necessarily an inner path into the secrets of the Self, and it is the path that mystics have walked for centuries.

86. Psychics and Shamans Tap into Spiritual Power

Psychics and shamans have traditionally been people who claim to sense the unseen, see into the future (divination), work with the supernatural in lower or higher realms of existence, or have the ability to influence unseen energies or spirits through spells, incantations, magic, dream work, music, ecstatic trances, and sacred dance. Ancient peoples called psychics and shamans by other names, medicine man/woman, priest/priestess, or sorcerer/sorceress, necromancer, and magician, for example, depending upon their particular cultures. Often shamans occupied places of high position within a village or culture.

87. How Shamans Have Used the Law of Attraction

To achieve the manifestation of the greater good, a spell might be cast, a blood-letting undertaken, a sacrifice made, or a dream incubated. For example, the shamans of several Native American tribes underwent vision quests, performed shamanic healings, sat in sweat lodges, and engaged in sun dances. They chanted incantations to ward off attacks by aggressive Europeans. That's not to say that they always got what they wanted because the law, when opposite poles of attraction are set up, responds to the more powerful vibrational pull or yields a less strong or, in some cases, a mixed result. Native Americans performed incantations but were still attacked and lost battles to their powerful enemies whose forces, goals, and intentions proved stronger.

88. Dreamtime of the Australian Aborigines

Alignment with the Law of Attraction, for the ancient Australian Aborigines, was alignment and access to the Dreamtime's energetic realm where they believed all creation takes place. Australian Aborigines were groups of people who migrated from the Asian continent to settle in Australia. Their tribes had various cultural practices but shared a deep reverence and connection to the land. Their view of the world's beginning was known as the Dreamtime and their shamans or sorcerers placed great emphasis on dreams, sand drawings, and music played upon a didgeridoo, among other instruments.

89. Spiritual Journeys and Aboriginal Manifestations

The Australian Aborigines went on "walkabouts" to a "belonging place" (sacred place in the landscape) where they sought access to the Dreamtime. In such practices, they could tap into a great power much as a Law of Attraction practitioner might move into harmonious alignment by undertaking a spiritual journey and specific meditation practice in order to manifest a desired result.

E. P. Elkin, an Australian anthropologist, called the aboriginal medicine men of Australia "men of High Degree" in his book *Aboriginal Men of High Degree,* and he admonished against devaluing the importance of their emphasis on psychic power as primitive magic.

90. Asian Shamans Touch the Spirit World

The ancient peoples of Tibet, Siberia, Laos, and elsewhere practiced shamanism, often within the context of their particular cultural belief system. As intermediaries between the world of matter and spirit, shamans were able to control malevolent spirits by accessing the spirit world, effect healings, and interpret dreams. Their special knowledge of the workings of the unseen world (alignment, surely, with the Law of Attraction) empowered them to deal with the invisible spirits or forces of misfortune that might be hurting those in their villages and bring out the manifestation of peace, health, and positive change for the greater good.

91. The Rise and Fall of the Aztec Empire

The Aztecs manifested the greatest and most powerful civilization of the Americas in central Mexico during the fourteenth century. The Aztecs aligned themselves with the Law of Attraction through their determination not only to survive but to prosper and become militarily strong. Their legacy of cities, pyramids, a Sun stone calendar, sacrificial platforms, and other architectural creations say much about their accomplishments and in-depth knowledge of mathematics and astronomy. And yet, the empire of the Aztecs completely disappeared.

Perhaps the element of violence within the Aztec culture through imposition of terror and tribute, ritual human sacrifices to their gods, and emphasis on extreme militarism created a vibration that eventually drew to them the demise of their civilization.

92. Ancient Magicians Possessed Mystical Knowledge

Magic is known to have existed in the Hellenistic society of the Greeks and Romans and mentions of magic in the Bible suggest that it was known within early Christian societies as well. The word "hermetic" is used to convey relevance to Hermes Trismegistus (known also as the Egyptian god Thoth and the Greek god Hermes) or the writings that have been ascribed to him, including alchemical, theosophical, astrological, and mystical doctrines.

Whether or not an ancient hermetic magician was cognizant of the workings of the Law of Attraction, he or she was assuredly engaged in practices with resolute intention and desire to draw forth a specific situation, event, and circumstance. Then as today, magicians utilized many devices and objects in their spells for good or for curses.

93. A Belief in Magic Can be Empowering

Magic may have emerged out of ancient religions in response to a need for individual empowerment by people to deal with cultural and societal pressures, concerns, and anxieties. Some suggest that the practice of magic enabled people during ancient times to have a greater sense of self while simultaneously revitalizing their spiritual and religious beliefs. Magicians were considered powerful individuals in their society and some even had followings.

Hermetic magic has been credited as being the forerunner of several magic and mystical orders as well as medieval alchemy in the western mystery tradition. The Hermetic path encompasses eclectic spiritual beliefs and even finds some resonance in pagan Gnosticism.

94. Everything is Constantly Evolving

Alchemy to the hermetic alchemists meant change/transformation. They were fascinated by change and their alchemical symbols, according to psychologist Carl Gustav Jung, have been welling up for centuries from the collective unconscious into sensitive souls. Jung spent the later years of his life fascinated by and absorbed in research on alchemy.

Hermetic alchemists were sometimes thought of as practitioners of black magic as they attempted to turn base metal into gold. They were seeking ways to speed up nature's evolutionary process, as they understood it. Metals were believed to be living things that were undergoing a process of change to become perfect—in short, to eventually become gold.

95. Intent Can Bring about Radical Transformation

Alchemy blurs the lines between science and philosophy, between the magical and the spiritual. But always, in the end, alchemy is about change/transformation. When a person desires to undertake personal growth work, he or she in some ways joins the ranks of ancient practitioners of magic or spiritual shamanism, for that person holds a deep desire to evolve and attempts to manifest the result through desire, intent, and action. Such transformation can bring a sea change in his or her relationships with others, for as psychologists point out: it only takes one person to shift a paradigm. In relationships, that means when the individual changes, everyone around that person necessarily has to change too.

CHAPTER 6

Steps You Can Take . . .
to Access Hidden Wisdom

96. Seek Wisdom from Many Sources

Through the ages, many people have turned to religion to search for wisdom about their life's meaning and purpose. Even the ancients understood that knowledge equates with power. During the Middle Ages, some who sought spiritual insight joined religious orders where higher learning was accessible. In the last century, seekers increasingly turned to Eastern philosophies. The decade of the seventies witnessed the use of "mind-expanding" drugs to enter alternative states of consciousness where they believed the secrets of the universe would become unconcealed. Today's wisdom seekers mine ancient traditions, science, and other sources.

97. Christian Mystics Understood the Law

The Law of Attraction works in the pursuit of spiritual desire just as it does for worldly things. Christianity emphasizes total submission of one's will to the will of God. Christian mystics have understood how the twin engines of faith and belief could merge the spiritual self into alignment and even unity with its Source. Some say that through divine grace they entered transcendental realms and moved closer to God.

Mystics of all religions have exhibited paranormal powers, gained knowledge and perceived truth through an inner knowing. That is not to say that all mystical experiences are pleasant. However, the understanding that mystics come away with from time spent in transcendental states have sometimes enabled them to manifest or create from spiritual desires (often to help others).

98. How Jesus Demonstrated the Law of Attraction

When Law of Attraction teachers speak of the power of faith, trust, belief, vision, and declaration, they frequently cite Jesus. Three of the New Testament gospels—Matthew, Mark, and Luke—attribute to Jesus the comment that the kingdom of heaven is like the least of all seeds (the mustard seed) that planted grows into the greatest of all herbs, a tree with branches to shelter the birds. Likewise, great accomplishments start with intent and small actions. When you nurture the seeds of divinity within, the Law of Attraction makes possible an unfolding of your spiritual consciousness and brings to you or guides you to the means to help yourself and others.

99. Faith Makes All Things Possible

In the Gospel of John, Jesus offers what has come to be known as the Sermon on the Vine and the Branches. A passage within that sermon has Jesus saying, "If ye abide in me, and my words abide in you, ye shall ask what ye will, and it shall be done unto you" (John 15: 7).

Living his life in tune with the purpose for which he had been sent to earth, Jesus showed through example how to love all, give much, believe all things are possible when your own power is aligned with God, and pray often with a heart of thankfulness.

100. Know that Divine Love is Reflected as Inner Joy

In *The Secret*, author Rhonda Byrne and her associates advocate seeking prosperity, abundance, inner joy, and peace and counsels that the job of each person is to decide what he or she wants. Mystics have always desired to draw nearer to God and to learn how to express His love to others.

That longing for the Divine has found resonance in the lives of Christian saints from the earliest days of the church. Indeed, the manifestation of the Divine in the physical world is represented by the myriad expressions of divine love. Jesus' words in the New Testament's Gospel of John encapsulate the depth of God's love.

101. Consider the Accomplishments of Teresa of Avila

Teresa of Avila was a medieval Spanish Carmelite nun whose desire for a deeper relationship with God eventually manifested as a result of her longing and effort. When she died, she left behind a rich legacy of devotional observations in her writings and her autobiography. Inspired by the Holy Spirit, Teresa yoked her desire to manifest a closer relationship with the Lord with intention and action, that is, her adherence to a physical life of strictest poverty and renunciation. Aligned in harmony with the Law of Attraction, she got what she wanted and more. In time, she shared her spiritual gifts through her books, *Life, The Way of Perfection*, and *The Interior Castle*.

102. Think Outside the Box

The Christian mystic Hildegard of Bingen experienced visions that started in childhood and continued until her death in 1179 A.D. During medieval times, women didn't keep journals nor jot down their spiritual or ecclesiastical ideas; however, Hildegard became convinced that she was being instructed by a heavenly voice telling her to record information gained during her ecstatic states of consciousness. Hildegard, worried that she might be ridiculed by others, was reluctant to do as she was told. Eventually, however, she began dictating to her scribe what her inner visions unveiled for her. She also created musical compositions, a morality play, poetry, and works of art that revealed what she called mysteries and secrets of the Divine. Her body of work earned her high regard by the church.

103. Your Inner World Can Be Made a Reality

Hildegard of Bingen perhaps exemplified the Law of Attraction's age-old idea that "as you think, so you become." Some might say that Hildegard's prodigious works during her lifetime sprang from an inner world in which her thoughts, observations, reflections, and mystical revelation found fecund ground. Her desire to serve the Lord meant following the instructions of a heavenly voice telling her to reveal her knowledge even though her fear of condemnation literally made her ill. Nevertheless, Hildegard worked in tune with her calling and perception of truth—all in alignment with deeply held spiritual beliefs, and the Law of Attraction ensured that her inner contemplative process bore even more fruit. Her desire to serve the Lord meant expressing the knowledge she was being given.

104. Project a Powerful Self-Image

Augustine of Hippo was endowed with a great mind and oratory skills, which he used in his service as a bishop in the early Christian church. He successfully manifested a powerful image of himself as an intellectually vibrant and powerful orator. He made the most of his genetic endowment for intellectual inquiry and oratory and was able to attract the means to further develop them. When Augustine deeply desired to overcome the sensual things of life that kept him from having a more personal relationship with God, he translated his desire into conviction and action. When the Law began to fulfill his desire for that experience, he wrote an intensely personal account of his struggle to come to terms with his sensual nature and to know God.

105. Obey Inner Guidance

In his book, *Confessions,* Augustine wrote that he came to God too late. He expressed regret that he had thrust himself upon the beautiful things that God had created instead of turning within to seek God, the Creator. According to *Confessions*, it was only after sensing a voice telling him to "take and read," was Augustine compelled to pick up a Bible where he read and obeyed a passage that instructed him to follow Christ. The Law of Attraction was at work at all times to give Augustine whatever he set his heart upon and felt driven to get—at first, stature as a hedonist and powerful orator and later, as a denunciate of hedonism and devoted follower of Christ.

106. Christians Debate the Law of Attraction

Many Christians are divided on whether or not the Law of Attraction aligns with Christian beliefs. Those against the Law assert that when people believe that they create their lives and everything in them, they diminish or eliminate God as Creator and practice self-deification. The claim that you can have ultimate knowledge and become godlike is what the serpent promised Eve in the Garden of Eden when tempting her to defy God's command to not eat from the tree of the knowledge of good and evil. Eve apparently formed a strong desire to have what the serpent promised her.

107. The Law May Be Part of God's Will

Eve ate the apple and offered some of it to her mate Adam. Some people feel strongly that only God creates and that humans desiring knowledge of universal laws and attempting to call upon the Universe to help them manifest or create their lives anew is putting the Universe before God. For some deeply devout Christians, the idea of creating a spiritual or religious life is admirable and credit should be given to the Lord. Others might say that the Lord's ways are mysterious and the Law of Attraction may be a divine mechanism to give people what they want, including drawing spiritually inspired souls closer to Him.

108. Choose to Pursue Wealth or Poverty

People in religious orders may take a vow of poverty but not a vow to acquire wealth and material possessions. Poverty has somehow always equated with deeply held spiritual aspiration whereas the pursuit of wealth often has been perceived as a selfish desire for things of the flesh instead of the spirit. The Law of Attraction, as you have already learned, is indifferent; it gives you whatever you think and feel you deserve. When you give yourself over to increase in your life, you are giving fuller expression to the abundance of the Divine Intelligence within you. However, if you seek poverty, the Law of Attraction will make it so. Proponents of the Law of Attraction say it is up to you to choose.

109. Believe and You May Be Healed

It is often difficult to assess whether or not an ill person has experienced a miraculous cure. Certainly doctors can attest to the recovery but explaining such a sudden (sometimes instantaneous) recovery in someone who has been diagnosed with a chronic affliction or terminal disease can be impossible. Still, many people do recover through the power of their faith and unshakable belief that they will become healthy again. When they have such faith and belief of having excellent health, they are setting up a powerful force for attracting recovery through the Law of Attraction. For a healing to be deemed miraculous, the church undertakes a thorough investigation to rule out other possible explanations. When there is no explanation, the person's cure is deemed a miracle.

110. Divine Power Works Miracles

Jesus served as a spiritual beacon—"I am come a light into the world . . . that whosoever believeth in me should not abide in darkness" (John 12: 46)—and an exemplar of how the power of God works through the human heart and mind. According to the New Testament

Gospels, Jesus performed many miracles that seemingly defied the natural laws of the universe. Among other things, he fed 5,000 people with five loaves and two fishes, exorcised demons, showed a mastery over nature by cursing the fig tree that then withered, raised the dead on three occasions, and healed sick people.

111. Sow Love and Reap Joy

The Hindu faith is rooted in ancient Vedic philosophy with its inherent ideas of karmic law or the law of retribution—what you sow, you reap; also, what you send out comes back. These ideas dovetail into the Law of Attraction because what you think about most is what you draw into your life experience. Throughout an average day in your life, are you thinking lovingly of the welfare of others or falling into a pattern of criticizing others for everything that makes you unhappy and stressed out? According to the tenets of Hinduism, your thoughts are as powerful as a spoken word. Words, like your actions, are creating your karma and when the elements are ripe for those words and actions to bear fruit (whether good or bad), they will.

112. Change Yourself to Change the World

Spiritual well-being for most Hindus comes as a result of living a clean and decent life, observing *ahimsa* or nonviolence, serving their families, performing *dharma* or their worldly duties and *sadhna* or spiritual practices in the right way, and showing respect for all life forms sacred things. Most Hindus are vegetarians. Also, they often place high value on selfless service to others. Respect for elders is culturally ingrained in most Hindus. A famous Hindu by the name of Mohandas Gandhi, the Father of India, once said that we must be the change that we seek in the world. Many Hindus seek to create a better world by first turning to the divine within to change themselves before trying to effect change in the world.

113. Exercise Mind over Matter

Certain Hindu yogis, sages, siddhis, and holy persons through the ages who have committed their lives to the pursuit of truth purportedly have been able to travel through time and space at will, shrink or expand in size, abstain from food and water without damage to their physical bodies, control their heartbeat and breath, effect miracle healings, and instantly produce tangible objects through the power of thought. Some sources say that the Law of Attraction finds resonance or has roots in tenets of Hinduism and shares the belief that an underlying unifying force of energy in the cosmos governs all that exists.

114. Do No Harm the Buddhist Way

Buddhist philosophy aligns beautifully with the Law of Attraction due to its emphasis on perception, thought, speech, and action. Right thought, for example, means to harm no person or thing through negative thought, including yourself, and to avoid desire and cravings and ill will. Instead, Buddhism emphasizes cultivating thoughts of goodwill, love, joy, and gratitude. Speech should never be critical, harsh, or malevolent, instead, it should be gentle, kind, truthful, and appropriate for time and place. Having a generosity of spirit and gratitude for the blessings you already have are as important in Buddhist practice as they are for deliberately working with the Law of Attraction.

115. Find a Balance of Yin and Yang

According to Taoist sage Lao Tzu, each person should find a balance between yin/yang. When faced with a problem, instead of responding with a knee-jerk aggressive action (yang), remain calm and find power and peace in the stillness. Then you will know the right course to the solution. Your thoughts often propel your body into action as a response to a problematic situation. Use your thoughts and the working of the Law of Attraction to draw to yourself solutions and opportunities by remaining in a quiet mindful (yin) place. That is the way of the Tao. You are neither advancing nor retreating. You are not buffeted about by emotions. Instead, you are anchored at the center of inner strength and power.

Steps You Can Take . . .

to Put the Law into Practice

116. Figure Out What You Really Want

If you like to shop, you will love the first step in Law of Attraction, which is to decide on what you want. How do you decide? Well close your eyes and think of something that you either want or need that would make you incredibly happy. Set aside your doubt and pretend for a moment that anything you want is possible. If doubt floods your mind, then just start small and continue taking baby steps in your manifesting efforts until you have proven to yourself how easy it is.

117. Beware of Indecision

Is what you want to manifest an object such as a new lipstick, a paella pan, a fountain for your garden? Is it situation you'd like to bring about such as improving your health, garnering a promotion, or mastering a tennis serve? Is it something you want to do for the world such as write a book, establish a business, or create a masterful work of art?

It's best to develop a crystal clear idea of the object of your desire and stick with it. Why? Because indecisiveness may render you some wild variant of what you really want.

118. Go Shopping in the Storehouse of the Universe

Think of how much you enjoy browsing through the pictures in your favorite catalogs or spending a day at the outlet stores or whiling away an hour or two at a Costco or Sam's Club warehouse. Now consider all the offerings of every store, merchant, or collective of all your favorite countries of the world. Remember, you are shopping in the warehouse of the universe. The promise of the law is that if you can imagine and desire something clearly enough, using high levels of creative energy, you can swiftly attract it.

119. Give Yourself Permission to Have What You Want

If you deny yourself permission to have the object of your desire, you will block its arrival. Reasons you might deny yourself permission to have something include feeling like you don't deserve it or your income doesn't support the purchase or you think someone else is more deserving. What you fervently desire is sure to manifest when you give yourself permission to have it, think about it often and with feeling, consider ways to acquire it, and set in motion the acquisition of it through your intent.

120. Desire Plus Intent Equals Your Dreams Come True

When you desire something deeply and form an intention to acquire it, you will begin to turn over in your mind ways that you might have the object of your desire. Intent to have something usually triggers strong emotional feelings such as excitement and happiness when you think about having the object. You feel motivated to work for it. When desire is coupled with intent and motivation, you begin to believe that you can attain the object you desire.

121. Maintain a Positive Attitude

Belief that you can have your desire must be sustained because there surely will be a period between dreaming of having it and the physical manifestation of it in your life. Seldom are manifestations instantaneous. Intensify your efforts of deliberately working with the Law of Attraction by feeling and expressing your thankfulness at what you already have. Feel gratitude also for the power that is working to bring you the object you fervently desire.

122. Clarify Your Intention

Clarity of intention brings faster and stronger results. Don't engage in wishful thinking and then forget about what you wanted. Be clear about your intention to have exactly what you want. Hold in your mind the image of your desired object. See the colors, the detailing, the size, the weight, and opacity or clarity, and even the timeframe in which you want it in your life. Do whatever you can to mentally see it in its totality. Think of all the ways it might arrive into your possession, how you will enjoy it, use it (wear it, drive it, etc.). Know with certitude that it is already in the universe on its way.

123. Change Your Energy if Necessary

If you don't like what you are attracting to yourself (negative friends, undesirable business situations or clients, loser boyfriends, and the like), change your energy. Clarify your intention to send out different vibrations and watch how the Law of Attraction will begin to bring you new friends, fantastic business associates and opportunities, even possibly a new romantic partner with qualities and moral values that you desire.

When your thoughts, emotion, and intention are aligned one hundred percent on achieving the optimal outcome, you will achieve greater success. Conversely, when you slide into a place of lower expectation and dilute the intention to have the best, then you may fail to achieve your desired goal.

124. Energize Your Intention

One way to energize intentional thought is by mapping out an action or to-do list. Think about some of the things you might do to set up a powerful magnetic attraction, drawing to you the object of your desire? Clean the garage, for example, to make possible a space to park that new sports car you want. Host a handbag party, cookware, or jewelry in which the hostess is given a gift depending on how many people attend the party. Your gift just might turn out to be the very item you desire. Throw a party and invite single people; ask everyone to bring a friend. Who knows, that new romantic partner you desire might just show up.

125. Be Open to Infinite Possibilities

By allowing your thoughts to frequently visit your desire and by opening your heart to feel positive emotions of joy and happiness around getting that desire, you are supporting your intention and strengthening the pull of the Law of Attraction. You are drawing toward you that which is already in infinite potentiality. But it bears repeating here that you must be vigilant about your thoughts. Negative situations, people, and objects drift into your life when you worry, fear, and feel stressful. But when you are happy, grateful, and feel empowered, more good things manifest such as healthy, loving relationships, a better job, and more money.

126. Use the Right Language

When asked about your desire, if you say, "I want to stop dating losers, you are putting yourself in position to continue attracting them. "Loser" is an emotionally potent word for people. It's so negative that it is the strongest word in that sentence. Find other words and phrasing to express your desire for a healthy relationship with an emotionally mature individual who is right for you. Think carefully about how you are asking for things. Instead of saying, "need to get out of this lousy job," try saying instead, "I am manifesting meaningful work in my field of [fill in the blank] that pays three times my current salary of [fill in the blank]," and I'll be working in that position by [fill in the date].

127. Always Look on the Bright Side

As the dark gets darker and more powerful, that's the best time to seek and generate light. Make yourself into a beacon of bright light and optimism. Express positive feelings and a grateful attitude for what's good in your life and let those feelings extend outward into the lives of all those you know and love. Don't give much energy to the things that aren't working for you. Try to be an observer in the drama and, as you seek whatever goodness you can find, watch how the energy begins to shift. At times, it can be positively palpable.

128. Demonstrate Generosity of Spirit

Generosity of spirit is symbolized by trust, mutual aid, kindness, and respect for others as well as doing as little harm as possible and assisting others in their journey through life. In short, the word "generosity" means the habit of giving and is often synonymous with charity. Cultivate generosity if you want to powerfully express and implement the Law of Attraction in your life. Give generously to receive generously. Be like the Hindu goddess Lakshmi, whose prayer states that the goddess is "generous to everyone." Her devotees rise early at dawn to chant the thousand names of the goddess with the intention of drawing into their lives her blessings of wealth.

129. Remember that Prosperity is for Everyone

Attracting wealth into your life does not mean that you are depleting someone else's reserve. Law of Attraction teachers and practitioners say that the power that brings something to you out of infinite potential can deliver the same thing to another. There is no corresponding loss to infinite potential. When you give from a place of loving kindness, your gift, some say, returns magnified many times over and sometimes in a different form.

130. Engage in Action Without Action

There is a concept in Taoism called "not doing" or *wu-wei*. In a discussion of generosity of spirit, *wu-wei* has a place because of its emphasis on living life from the spirit, expressing harmony and love in all you do. Andrew Carnegie demanded his employees work together in a spirit of harmony because he believed it was a critical important factor in achieving success. The power behind wu-wei's "action without action" is synchronicity. When you set forth an intent or desire in your mind and are harmoniously aligned with the energy of the Tao, your power, invisible and strong, works with the laws of the universe.

CHAPTER 8

Steps You Can Take . . .

to Reinforce Your Intent

131. Understand the Role of Emotions

An effective reinforcement tool for working with the Law of Attraction is an understanding of how your mood affects your ability to attract the results you desire. It may be more difficult than you think to understand how external and internal thoughts can trigger feelings that translate to good or bad moods. Yet such knowledge can be a powerful aid in your manifestation efforts. You'll know what your mood triggers are and recognizing them can help you to quickly redirect when you slip into a negative mood or reinforce a positive one.

132. Be Aware of Your Moods

Mood is the best indicator of your emotion. The happiness you feel when doing work you love and feel passionate about can quickly change into hurt when someone criticizes you. You may even become angry and desire to lash out at that person. In a short span of time, you've just experienced three emotions.

Everyone feels emotions as various bodily sensations. In a dangerous situation, you may feel the "fight or flight" response due to your body's sudden release of adrenalin. People behave according to the emotions they are feeling in their bodies, and there are many personality disorders that have an emotional component.

133. Recognize the Social Emotions

Any emotion can affect the way you make decisions. Another group of emotions known as social emotions include pride, jealousy, guilt, and embarrassment. Negative emotions, such as anger or fear, along with any self-defeating thoughts can keep you from taking advantage of opportunities when they show up in your life. Psychiatrists say that anger turned inward (internalized) can become depression and that emotion can surely paralyze the decision-making process. Sharpening your understanding of social emotions and when you feel them can be a powerful tool in your box of attraction and manifestation aids.

134. Consider How Emotions Affect Your Decisions

Grief, fear, hopelessness, shame, and disgust can also render you unable to logically reason through all the factors to effectively make a sound decision. When it comes to deciding to manifest something in your life, making the decision to do so is easier than making a life and death decision because of the anticipatory feelings associated with getting something you desire.

If you are in a bad mood and are asked to decide something, you are likely to revisit negative memories and anticipate negative consequences to your decision. However, if you are in a good mood when asked to make a decision, you may anticipate a positive outcome to your answer based on your good feelings instead of arriving at a nonemotional decision made purely on reasoning and logic.

135. Take Other Feelings into Account

When you feel strong visceral sensations like hunger, pain, or sexual desire, or crave a substance like alcohol, for example, powerful neurophysiologic mechanisms may be driving those feelings.

Likewise your subconscious fears, needs, and wants color how you experience life and make decisions when the future outcome is uncertain. Decision-making is often done in the presence of thoughts about whether the decision will generate benefit or harm in your life.

The "fight or flight" response is a biological stress response to fight or flee when there is the perception of eminent threat. Think of a caveman resting under a tree who suddenly spots a deadly cobra in threatening posture. The man's sympathetic nervous system releases adrenaline and stress hormones to rapidly adapt to such a dangerous situation.

136. Aim for a Healthy Expression of Emotion

Mental health professionals say that it is unhealthy to suppress your emotions. Instead, you are encouraged to express feelings in positive ways in order to process through them. Getting to the root of anger, for example, is an important precursor to working with the Law of Attraction because once you know what triggers it you can deal with the cause and then forgive and release. Working on your self-esteem proves easier once old issues have been resolved. It's important that you feel worthy and deserving of the good things in life and that you develop a success consciousness. Your brain is the most powerful manifestation tool you have. It needs care and attention for it to perform its role in working with the Law of Attraction.

137. Expect to See Your Desires Fulfilled

Expecting to receive what you desire is vital to getting it. A heightened sense of expectation intensifies the vibration of your thought whenever you dare to expect that the thing, person, or circumstance you desire is yours to be had. Allowing yourself to feel a sense of expectation reinforces the attraction or pull of it to you. Expectation evolves into a sense of anticipation when you believe so strongly that what you desire is on its way to you that you accept it without doubt. Pleasure levels rise within you. You are excited, anticipatory, and happy. Replace patterns of thinking such as self-doubt or self-criticism with appreciation of your body and mind. Practice self-forgiveness, self-patience, self-understanding, and self-love.

138. Remember How it Feels To Get What You Want

When your anticipatory feelings of expectation coincide with the actual event finally occurring, a heightened state of pleasure sets in. Think of a time when something wonderful happened to you. When you recall that experience, how do you feel? Happy again? Now think about something you deeply desire that you know at some point is going to show up in your life, for example, getting a promotion with a huge pay increase, finding the love of your life, conceiving a child, receiving a scholarship, or buying your dream house. The happiness grows in intensity, doesn't it?

139. Test Your Emotional Ability

Close your eyes and imagine a tragic event (the loss of a loved one, the hurt of rejection, the suffering of a pet or your child, for example). Think of a future event that could also make you heavy-hearted. If you felt your eyes welling with tears, a lump in your throat, heaviness in your chest, and unmistakable waves of sadness washing over you, the good news is that you will also likely be able to feel the opposite emotion of happiness, joy, and delight.

You can call up a negative emotion; examine where it came from, try to understand what it might be teaching you, and expiate it from your subconscious in numerous ways, including EMDR (eye movement desensitization reprocessing), self-hypnosis, dream work and lucid dreaming, art therapy, mask-making, and other self-help methods.

140. Prepare for Limitless Potential

The limits of your abilities, according to many psychologists, are based on your limiting beliefs. The good news is that you can challenge those beliefs and replace them with more empowering beliefs about yourself. Think of cutting a new groove in your brain that allows your imagination to stretch and set goals that you may have once believed unattainable. Then let your thoughts create the optimum environment for manifesting those goals from the storehouse of the Universe.

141. Make Use of Self-Help Tools

The average person uses only about five to ten percent of her mind, mostly for thinking, feeling, reasoning, and storing memories. With the aid of some techniques for developing creativity and intuition along with other New Age tools such as lucid dreaming, psychic development, and energy manipulation for healing, yoga, meditation, and communication with higher consciousness, among others, you could use more of your mind for self-discovery, innovative and new ideas, and personal growth.

142. Examine Your Thought Processes

You have the power to intensify that attraction through a variety of ways already discussed, including the use of music, visualizations and other visual cues, declarations and incantations, spells, dream incubations, and affirmations. If you find that your affirmations are not working for you, do a little self-introspection. Are you spending five minutes each day affirming and the other twenty-three hours and fifty-five minutes in negative self-talk or doubtful "reality" mode, try flipping the equation.

Affirming the belief that what you desire is in the process of coming to you is the best way to deflect doubt when it creeps in. Trust what you want is on its way, and give thanks for that. Sidestep the details of how and when it's coming. Let Source handle those. You focus on reinforcing desire and intention through all means available.

143. Make it a Habit

Bad habits such as overindulgence in food or drink, chronic tardiness, lack of focus, and avoidance issues when faced with a problem can screw up every area of your life. Overlay your bad habits with good ones. Make a commitment to repeat the good habit until it takes hold, displacing and eventually replacing the bad one.

Habitually focus on having abundance, rather than lack in your life. Establish a routine of setting aside certain times throughout the day to consider the abundance that already exists in your life. Discover what makes you feel alive and passionate. Pursue that and the Universe will support you. Count your blessings and feel grateful while also having the expectation that your desires await your beckoning through your emotionally charged positive thinking.

144. Trust the Universe

Establish the intention to manifest your desire with goals and then magnetize your intention with confidence and certitude of achieving positive results.

Allow your mind to wrap around your desire and all the various possibilities of ways you can help the Law of Attraction bring that person, circumstance, or thing into your life. It doesn't hurt to develop specific goals and ideas about opportunities to watch for in order to attain your desire but don't get too bogged down with how your desire can manifest. That limits the Universe's options in bringing it to you. Don't forget to consider why you want to manifest your desire, what you will do with it, and how it will make you feel.

145. Get Ready for the Object of Your Desire

Cultivate conviction and make ready to receive. Know with your heart, mind, and soul that the object of your desire is en route to you at this very moment. Allow the object to come into your life. Because the destiny of the object of your desire is to be claimed by you, practice seeing yourself having it. Let yourself experience joy and the satisfaction of finally having your desire wash over you again and again.

Develop an attitude of gratitude and express appreciation often. Allow yourself to feel like you have forever been and always will be in the protective and capable hands of the Divine. Let go of all worry and feel serene, peaceful, happy, and grateful.

146. Eliminate Negative Messages

Reduce the amount of negativity you will tolerate. Americans are bombarded daily by advertising messages that emphasize dissatisfaction and lack in each person's life. Some sources say that the average person receives more than a thousand negative messages daily such as "you need a better mattress," "you need a sleeker, faster car," "you need to switch your hair color product," or "you need the purple pill to salvage your sex life." Ask yourself how you eliminate negative messages in order to raise your level of life satisfaction.

147. Use Positive Thinking to Change Your Life

Engaging in positive thinking certainly makes our lives more pleasurable than living day to day persistently engaging in negative thinking. One positive thought is likely to generate another, creating a cycle. The steady stream of thoughts will flow, whether or not you direct it. The happy and good life, that sometimes seems so elusive to some, can become reality with a simple redirecting of thought, say experts on the Law of Attraction. Positive thinking and goal setting, working in concert, are now considered scientifically viable methods for changing a person's life. You can impress upon your subconscious the belief that positive thinking brings you the good things you desire in life. In that way, habitual positive thinking yields faster results.

CHAPTER 9

Steps You Can Take . . .
to Avoid Negativity

148. Remember that Negative Thoughts Can be Harmful

Perhaps you know from direct experience the impact of negativity. For example, maybe you have had the experience of happily going off to work only to sink into a foul mood an hour later because a coworker, who never let a negative thought go unspoken, decided this was the morning she would unload her burden on you. Negativity is both malignant and infectious. It is difficult to have mental clarity and a positive outlook so necessary for intentional alignment with the Law of Attraction when you are in such an environment.

149. Don't Let Negative Thoughts Hijack Your Mind

Mulling over a problem in order to come up with creative solutions is one thing, but when fear triggers the emotional part of the brain, worrying takes over . . . often obsessively. The worrying mind attracts more negative situations to worry about. Experts in behavior and brain science warn that worrying can overshadow and negate reason and logic.

In his book *Emotional Intelligence, Why It Can Matter More than IQ*, author Dr. Daniel Goleman asserts that while anxiety weakens the intellect and undercuts all types of mental and academic performances, a positive mood, especially one in which laughter is expressed, can facilitate flexible and complex thinking.

150. Recall the Power of Language

When you are in a bad mood and your mental thought vibration is negative, you use words like "no," "not," "can't," "won't," "don't," and "impossible." But when you feel upbeat and happy, you use positive expressions like "yes," "can," "will," "do," and "possible." When you say "can't," "won't," "don't," and "no," you are giving your thought attention on what you do not want because the mind sifts the negative contractions out of the statement and focuses on what remains. Try substituting a positively phrased question like "What is my deepest desire and in my best interest?" Then express what you want using positive language and avoiding those negative words. Give focused attention and energy to your positive affirmation statements.

151. Steer Clear of Negative Words and Phrases

When you say an affirmation that resonates with you, your affirmation becomes positive. But when you make a desire declaration that is not true for you, your feeling is conflicted because you have doubts that it can really be true. Doubt cancels out your desire and blocks manifestation.

Clarity of desire and the absence of any doubt are of paramount importance in getting what you want from the Universe. If necessary, write a list of what you *don't* want so that when you write your desire of what you do want, you can write it without obfuscation and words that evoke a negative vibration. You'll know by how you feel if what you've declared is true for you. You will feel relieved, possibly joyful, hopeful, and excited.

152. Eliminate Blockages with Positive Thought Energy

When the law takes too long or doesn't seem to work as you had hoped, you can assume that there may be blockages or obstacles that need clearing. Check your thought patterns. Are you experiencing skepticism, fear, anxiety, doubt, or worry? Check your feelings. Remedy blockages by asserting control over your conscious mind. Become quiet and permit your higher self or Divine Mind to take charge in quelling your mind's constant chatter.

Some spiritual seekers who regularly spend time chanting a specific mantra each day have been known to awaken from a dream and remember that within the dream they had been chanting the same mantra, suggesting that repetitious verbalization or mental thought can be impressed upon the subconscious and emerge in the dreaming mind.

153. Eliminate Subconscious Doubt

You can exert control over your conscious thoughts to some degree, but your subconscious may be a wee bit more challenging. You may have the urge to declare that you can't possibly be responsible for any negative thinking that goes on in your subconscious but the fact is that no one *but* you is responsible. It is, after all, your mind. Don't blame your parents, ex-husband, or others. Use frequent affirmations and creative visualizations to eliminate doubt and negative emotions that can block your alignment with the workings of the law.

154. Strengthen Your Desire by Journaling

If you are using personal affirmations, visualizations, and emotional magnetizing of your thoughts and you still feel blocked, try journaling your visualizations. From your visualization exercise, write down everything you observed with your mind's eye. Feel the positive emotions that come up for you when you read over your script. Record all the specific details as well as your feelings. Make your visualization and the journal entry as complete as possible.

Now take time to put everything together; that is, write, read, and recite a personal desire declaration and an affirmation. Make it true for you. Visualize your desire. Notice your positive emotions. Write about your visualization exercise in your journal. Allow the space in your life for the desire to manifest. When your desire comes into your life, that is, manifests, be appreciative and bask in feelings of elation, satisfaction, fulfillment, and gratitude.

155. Don't be a Victim of Your Own Negative Thoughts

The Universe or Source has already given each person everything he or she needs in the form of consciousness and universal laws to be the creator of his or her own destiny. Creative manifestation simply requires an individual claiming that which he desires. People who complain about their misfortunes or illnesses or lack bring more of that to themselves. They are victims of their own patterns of habitual negative thinking.

Work with your mind to make it into a powerful instrument on which you know you can always depend. The mind, properly trained against its tendencies to fall into the same ruts of thought, the same lazy patterns of self-criticism, can be your most powerful ally in whatever undertaking strikes your fancy.

156. Make Statements that Are True for You

If you have a pattern of attracting unhealthy relationships but you make a desire declaration that you have healthy and loving relationships in your life, you won't attract them because you know deep down that it isn't currently true for you. Focus on feeling and nurturing statements that can be spoken as true for you and focus on your desire as being "in process" and occurring right now: "I love that I am attracting . . ." or "I feel excited that I am . . ." or "I love the thought of . . ."

157. Understand How Doubt Blocks Manifestation

You have formulated a clear desire. You feel fantastic every time you declare it. However, if you have doubt (the uncertainty that you can truly attract your desire to you), that doubt or limiting belief evokes a negative vibration and will cancel out the positive statement of your desire. Eliminate the doubt and rework your desire declaration until it rings true and makes you feel happy and excited.

Perhaps the most important step in deliberate manifesting is the art of allowing something to come into your life. Believe that you deserve it and are worthy and ready to receive. Let your desire come in.

158. Break the Cycle of Negative Thinking

Quiet observation of your thoughts will shed light on how much of your inner dialogue is negative in response to internal thoughts or external stimuli. Statements such as "I don't have time," "I can't help it," or "I can't afford it" are self-limiting. You remember an old hurt, and the negative feelings are now there in the present. You see a coat in the department store window and want it but it costs too much. You feel bad. Such instant reactionary responses must be subdued and eventually replaced with positive responses.

159. Focus on Positive Feelings

To create a positive statement for a desire declaration, focus on feeling. For example, "I feel excited that I have all the time I need" or "I am thrilled to know that my talents are in demand in the marketplace and I am attracting the perfect job" or "I am attracting into my life ideal friendships that are vibrant, healthy, nurturing, and stimulating" or "I love feeling abundant and knowing that money easily flows to me from myriad sources." These kinds of declarative statements establish desire linked with positive feelings and in the present moment.

160. Contemplate the Patterns that Reveal Self-Limiting Beliefs

Years of self-limiting beliefs may be sabotaging you without your realizing it. These beliefs reveal themselves in patterns that keep coming up again and again in your life. Limiting beliefs often are so ingrained that they may seem to be at the heart of who you are—the very core of your being.

Self-limiting beliefs hold you back from most personal and spiritual growth. Perhaps you have engaged in self-sabotage, working hard to achieve something only to undermine your hard work with persistent, self-defeating inner criticism. With the Law of Attraction, you can have success and abundance and you do not have to suffer to achieve it. You do have to recognize and release self-limiting beliefs.

161. Don't be Afraid to Defy Logic

Proponents of the Law of Attraction assert that every person can create a life of wealth, abundance, and happiness that otherwise might seem improbable or impossible and defies logic and reason. If a review of your life and the goals you had established make you feel happy, it's likely you accomplished them. On the other hand, if you feel sad or disappointed, you likely did not accomplish them.

If you feel stuck or trapped, set goals for various areas of your life—spiritual, health, family, work, personal. List specific reasons that keep you from reaching your goals (include what has stopped you in the past). Know that you have to power to release even the most ingrained beliefs and turn them around into affirmations of unlimited potential.

162. Let Your Excitement Build Momentum

When you do spiritual work, you must learn surrender and become listener of the voice within. Surrendering to that inner wisdom allows you to know with a kind of knowing that goes beyond logical thinking. Likewise, when you work with the Law of Attraction, you must set aside logic and reason, curry trust and faith, and know with an inner knowing that the Law works. When the Law gives you even a little indication that it is working (through synchronicity or sending you signs), you will feel excited and your belief will be reaffirmed. Your excitement increases your joyful vibration, which, in turn, increases your level of trust in the Law.

163. Keep a Law of Attraction Journal

It is helpful to have a place to record your desire declarations, affirmations, visualizations, statements of evidence or proof (that the Law has manifested some part or all of your desires), and prayers or statements of gratitude. Include in your pages images of your desires and dreams. As your desires manifest, place a symbol that has meaning for you upon your written declaration in your journal. In fact, make a note each time positive things flow easily into your life. Rejoice. When you rejoice and commemorate each manifestation, your vibration aligns with the law to bring you even more abundance.

164. Give the Law Space to Work

Perhaps your desire has many steps that seem to boggle your mind when you ponder how much must be done in order for that dream or goal to manifest. Your work is not to figure out how the Law of Attraction has to work to manifest. Your job is to create the vibration around your desire and intention and to stay in harmonious alignment with the working of the Law. The Law of Attraction will do the rest.

165. Beware of Negative People

When you are feeling happy and positive and suddenly someone with a dark and negative vibration visits you, you most likely will feel a palpable energy shift downward. Instead of staying in the lower vibration, remind yourself of what is in your best interest. You may need to leave the company of that individual in order to again feel happy and positive.

A yogic technique for ridding yourself of a bad habit, such as being judgmental or overly critical of yourself or others is to close your eyes and focus your attention at the point between the eyebrows. Don't strain but focus gently and affirm the new good habit. Keep thinking about it until it becomes ingrained. Reinforce it daily.

166. Develop a Higher Vibration

The higher your level of emotion and belief, the higher your vibration and the more likely you will swiftly attract into your life the ideal romantic relationship, more abundance, spiritual understanding, vibrant health, financial prosperity, meaningful work, or other desire. Since self-limiting thoughts and doubt slows or blocks the arrival of your goals manifesting, keep your energy and emotions high and use everything you have learned thus far to stay in alignment with the law.

167. Activate Your Subconscious

As you learned earlier in this chapter, the Law of Attraction won't bring into existence something that you may be repeatedly affirming but do not really believe you can have. By asking "how can I have this," you are activating the amazing powers of your subconscious to provide solutions and opening the way for the Law of Attraction to work.

Great ideas may begin percolating through your mind or you begin to see opportunity everywhere because of your positive mental attitude and elevated vibration. Solutions or plans to circumvent obstacles may unexpectedly emerge.

Steps You Can Take . . .

to Improve Your Health

168. Use Positive Energy to Promote Health and Longevity

Modern experts in alternative medicine now assert what shamans and spiritual healers perhaps have always known—that the power of an optimistic mind can often heal the ailments of the body. It's well known that optimists live longer than pessimists. If you can accept that, at your most fundamental level, you are an energy being and that energy attracts like energy, you can begin to deliberately manifest good health. The Law of Attraction is always at work to bring you what you believe is true about your body and its health.

169. Master the Needs of Your Body

If you want to get healthy and stay that way, start with healthy thoughts. Paramahansa Yogananda, founder of the Self-Realization Fellowship wrote in *The Divine Romance* that sickness and health are both dreams of the mind. Cultivate joy, tranquility, optimism, and a sense of wonder. Laugh a lot since laughing has been proven to produce health benefits. Become childlike in your view of life, nature, and the wonders that already exist around you. Minimize the amount of pessimism, doubt, and worry you allow yourself to experience. Do not be enslaved by the whims, desires, and demands of the body. Take care of it, but be its master.

170. Implement Healthy Thinking

Cultivate feelings of self worth. Think about how you felt at a time when you were at the peak of good health. Ask yourself what brought about the decline in your health. Is it something that can remain in the past or is it still a factor? If it is still a factor, what can you do to get rid of it or minimize its impact? How committed are you to improving your health, stamina, and overall well-being? What steps will you take in the next moment, hour, or day to get on the road to good health? Remember, poor health can attract other problems and even shorten your life expectancy. Every thought you think, every act you do to achieve good health can bring huge health benefits and, in some cases, extend longevity.

171. Change Your Thoughts to Improve Your Health

Find ways to engage your mind in interesting endeavors. A healthy mind is an engaged mind. For example, your mind is stimulated when you endeavor to learn how to speak a new language, play a musical instrument, and do crossword or Sudoku puzzles. A healthy mind also focuses on positive rather than negative thought patterns. Perhaps you have noticed in your own life linkage between periods of positive thought patterns and feelings of wellness versus negative thinking and maladies.

172. Employ Tools of Healing

You can use sound healing, aromatherapy, massage, breath work, herbal and hydro therapies, massage, and guided meditation for mind/body healing. They are techniques found in virtually every medical tradition, including the ancient health teachings of Ayurveda, and increasingly Western-trained physicians may include those therapies along with medications and other conventional treatments. People working deliberately with the Law of Attraction may gain increased benefit from such treatments because of their optimistic outlook for improvement of their conditions.

Mind/body medicine is also referred to as behavioral medicine. Formerly labeled fringe medicine by conservative academic and medical establishments, mind/body medicine in recent times has gained such wide public support (one recent study showed that one in three adults have used alternative therapies) that the National Institutes of Health have established the Office of Alternative Medicine.

173. Plant the Seeds of Good Karma

The Tibetan Buddhist approach to healing necessarily begins in the mind. The Buddhist philosophy teaches that the mind is the creator of all problems and remedies, good fortune and bad, health and sickness. Buddhists believe in the law of karma. Each person is constantly sowing karmic seeds that persist until the right circumstances occur to cause the seeds to bear their karmic fruit. Negative karma manifests as problems, disease, and suffering while positive karma shows up as success, good fortune, and vibrant health. To the degree that you can control your emotions and thought patterns, you can influence your karma and, thus, your health and vitality.

174. Practice Mindfulness

Mindfulness means being present in each moment and noticing the quality of your thoughts even as you are being observant. Standing sentinel at the doorway of your consciousness to guard against creating seeds of negative thought (which, in turn, creates negative karma, according to Buddhism) is the way to avert sickness of the body and mind. The Buddhist philosophy states that you must avoid any action that is harmful to yourself or others and that you remain vigilant in monitoring your thoughts. In that way, you avoid attracting ill health to yourself in this life as well as in any future incarnations. Negative thoughts, words, and actions are like poison arrows that once sent out are destined to return to the sender.

175. Learn to Be in Harmony with Your Body

You won't reap all the positive benefits of exercise if you resent having to do it and are fuming the entire time you are walking, swimming, or cycling. Align your expectation and desire with the Law of Attraction if you want good health, for what your mind believes and expects about your body and its mental, emotional, and physical condition is what it receives more of.

Accept and appreciate your body. Think of it as your friend. Instead of constantly criticizing how you feel or look, decide on what positive things you can do the effect the changes you desire. When illness comes, don't think of the body as betraying you. Work with your body to rid itself of wrong thinking and feeling.

176. Breathe Your Pain Away

A simple technique to help relieve pain in a sore muscle involves attentive breathing. If you have pain in your leg while doing yoga, for example, focus your conscious mind like a laser upon the painful area, breathe in and imagine the painful tension as a dark hard knot breaking up into a gazillion pieces under the energy of your attention. Breathe out, releases the broken pieces of the knot. See them coalescing as a dark cloud that floats away to the horizon and disappears. Keep doing the technique until the pain subsides or completely dissipates.

177. Abandon Selfishness

While self-love and self-respect are necessary for self-esteem, obsessive self-focus and selfishness can cause you to think and act in ways that can be detrimental to your health and well-being. The seeds of selfishness often sprout into anger, greed, and jealousy that, in turn, can fuel feelings of haughtiness or superiority over other beings. In Buddhist thought, selfishness is the root cause of all problems and disease. When you feel hostility, you attract more of it to you.

178. Transform Your Thoughts

Another Buddhist idea is the transforming of negative thought or labels into positive ones. For example, when a doctor pronounces that you have a disease, you may react to his labeling of your affliction with fear, horror, and helplessness. You may see the disease as a problem, but you could also see it as a positive element in your life, the fruition of some karmic seed and the means to consciously alter your lifestyle in order to live in more balanced and spiritual ways. You could work on developing a compassionate mind. The transformation of negative thoughts into positive ones can effect changes in the body, restoring health. The body is, after all, is our physical dwelling.

179. Explore the Magical World Within

Imagination is much more powerful than reason. The magical kind of thinking that goes on in the imagination addresses the subconscious mind, which is childlike with respect to how it does not question directives that are both simple and repetitive, for example, an affirmation that your left knee is in the process of healing so you can again dance the tango or that your eyesight is becoming stronger to better see the veins of wildflowers, or that your body is growing more muscular, healthy, and better proportioned like a Greco-Roman goddess or another image that appeals to you. To stimulate the mind's fantasizing abilities, use colorful imagery rather than dry data and facts.

180. Be Well and Stay Well

According to principles of the Law of Attraction, the key to a long and healthy life lies in what you believe about yourself. According to some scientific studies and cultural beliefs, lifestyle choices and genetic factors are not the only indicators for longevity and health. Your dad may have lived to see his hundredth birthday or your mother perhaps died of breast cancer in her early forties, but that does not mean that you will have the same fate. Here are some ways to get healthy: eat right, get plenty of rest, quit smoking, and follow your doctor's advice before undertaking a regimen of exercise, but also remember the healing power of the mind. Your optimistic outlook, positive thinking, and reduction of stress should make up part of a regular regimen for becoming healthy and staying that way.

181. Reduce Your Stress Level

Stress can be a good thing inasmuch as it triggers alertness when we need it, for example, giving a speech or performing for others, and stress also prepares us to react instantly to danger. During a healthy stress response, norepinephrine, an excitatory neurotransmitter that is necessary to create new memories, is released.

Everyone feels stress from time to time, but unrelenting stress, the kind that you might experience in a high pressured job, without any reduction or relief, can wreak havoc on your health. According to several sources, including WebMD.com, seventy-five to ninety percent of all doctor's visits may be attributed to stress-related ailments and costs the U.S. economy in excess of $300 billion annually.

182. Revise Your To-Do List

Make a list of all the things you do each day. Prioritize your list into things that only you can do and work you can delegate to others. Of the things only you can do, reorder the list so that the most critical things (and likely most stressful) are spaced out with other tasks that may also be critical but that you love to do. The point is to create balance between work you dread and work you love. Evaluate how you feel after a day of using the new list to see if you managed to reduce your high levels of anxiety and stress.

183. Learn to Set Boundaries and Resolve Conflicts

Highly successful athletes understand (either consciously or intuitively) how to work with the Law of Attraction. They understand the role that a positive attitude plays in goal achievement. They deal with a potentially stressful situation immediately (putting off resolution allows the stress to continue building), set professional and personal boundaries and goals, and, though competitive, usually display good sportsmanship in competition. That means they learn how to engage in healthy conflict resolution—all of which aid in stress reduction. When you cannot establish firm boundaries or say no to others' demands, you may feel that people such as coaches, friends, business associates, or family members are treading all over you. As a result, you may harbor feelings of hostility and resentment.

184. Take Time to Release Stress

Set aside a little time every day to release the cumulative stressful feelings you have taken on throughout your day. Release the tension. Put on some quiet music or sit or lie quietly and just be aware of your breath. Let go of tension with every outgoing breath. Feel appreciation and joy for the gift of life and for a functioning body that is your vehicle for this incarnation. Be grateful in the knowledge that it is in your power to create vibrant health.

185. Practice Healthy Body Visualization Techniques

Do you see yourself as too thin, fat, disproportional, flabby, old, wrinkled, weak, frail, wracked with pain, or coming down with something? Such messages may or may not be true, but you can change your health and sense of well-being by changing your thoughts and raising your vibration. Your thoughts are magnetized by feeling so if you are feeling that you are weak, you cannot attract strength; if you feel that you are flabby and fat, you cannot draw to you lean and thin; and if you feel a cold is coming on, it probably will. Conversely, if you feel lithe, strong, and full of energy, you attract those qualities when you frequently give them your attention and feeling of appreciation.

186. Heal Illness and Dis-Ease through Positive Affirmations

The statement, "thoughts are things," finds repetition in New Age circles and at Law of Attraction seminars. A passing thought about diabetes might not cause the condition to manifest, but if you constantly worry and fear that you're going to develop it, you just might. Then what? How do you reverse the process, get rid of the illness?

If you want perfect health, affirm it by proclaiming that you want it and that you like the way your body feels when it is healthy. The beings known as Abraham in the Hicks' book, *The Law of Attraction, The Basics of the Teachings of Abraham* have stated that thinking such thoughts make you feel good and such feeling places you in tune with the Law to attract perfect health.

187. Let Your Body Heal Itself

When you let go of destructive patterns, release victimology thinking, take responsibility for your choices in life and the consequences, and forgive, you will be taking a giant step toward healing whatever ails you. For dis-ease is just that—the lack of ease about your life, your body, your choices . . . whatever troubles your mind and heart and brings discord to your life. Have patience with your body. Allow the wisdom of the cells to work. Just as the body knows how to mend a broken bone, it also knows how to heal cancer and other scourges of the body considered "incurable" by the vast majority of people.

188. Don't Dwell in Fear

In working with the Law of Attraction, you need not dwell on what initially caused the problem nor worry about when the condition initially emerged. Your work is to believe that the condition or illness is gone and vibrant health has returned. Just by feeling good, you are in touch with the energy source of all that exists, say some Law of Attraction teachers, and that high frequency energy source is your lifeline to a lifetime of good health.

Steps You Can Take . . .

to Attain Wealth

189. Stop Focusing on What You Lack

Perhaps the only area of your life where you are experiencing lack is in the money sector. You may feel that the American Dream is passing you by. The only abundance you seem to be manifesting is debt—college loans, credit cards, mortgage and car payments. There never seems to be an extra quarter, much less a dollar, left over at the end of the month. At times, you feel beaten. You wonder if you'll ever get ahead. What you might be doing is blocking the flow of money into your life by your worries about your indebtedness. Concentrate not on your unfortunate circumstances but rather on the good things that are now en route to you through the Law of Attraction.

190. Imagine Yourself Attracting Money

It's difficult to go from a poverty mentality to an abundance mindset, but that's what you have to do. Set aside a few minutes whenever possible to visualize yourself (literally) as a money magnet. Feel excited, jubilant, and elated—the way you would feel if you won the lottery. Visualize money flying to you from myriad sources, both known and unknown. Allow your thoughts to consider how you might create new income streams. Without giving into the impulse to hoard your newfound money, focus on ways to begin building wealth. You may think it's impossible to acquire and grow wealth, but it's not. You have abundant universe to support and provide for you and an invisible creative power to call upon.

191. Get Your Money Flowing

Start moving the energy of abundance by creating flow. You create flow by giving to others what you desire (for example, love, money, appreciation) and doing so without thought of lack or deprivation. Live from a sense of abundance rather than lack. Know that money is energy that must move or circulate. Be grateful for each nickel, dime, and dollar as it comes to you and remember to give something back to others. Those old sayings by Benjamin Franklin and others, "a penny saved is a penny earned" and "give more, get more" don't cancel each other out; they are part of the cycle of the circulation of money.

192. Give What You Need

If you go to the grocery store and a bell ringer for charity stands outside when you leave, drop some coins into the charity bucket. Mentally affirm that the money will return to you many times over to help you build financial prosperity for yourself and your family.

This giving what you desire to manifest more of in your life is an important concept. If you want money, give money; if it's love or respect then show love and respect to others. If you are stingy in your giving, don't be surprised if only a little money flow trickles back. Your gift, however, is less important than your attitude about living an abundant life—giving and believing that you will always have more to give. Of itself, that is a powerful positive affirmation.

193. Adopt the Millionaire Mindset

Financial success comes even more quickly when you do the following three things: imagine your monetary desire with strong intention to manifest it, frequently put purposeful attention on your goals (for example, to draw to you $5,000 dollars from sources known and unknown over the next month), and be involved actively in achieving your desired outcome (be on the lookout and take advantage of new opportunities to create income streams and also open to allowing the universe to bring you what you want). Your thoughts about abundance or lack of money create a vibration that magnetizes your mindset. That magnetic vibration either impedes or enhances the flow of currency to you.

194. Think about What Abundance Means to You

Abundance means different things to different people. For some, abundance is having the good things in life that money can't buy and for others it is financial freedom. For someone who has survived a natural disaster like the Hurricane Katrina or tsunami in Thailand, lived under a tyrannical dictator, or escaped a war zone, abundance means something different than it might mean to an individual trying to raise three kids alone and having to work two jobs to do it. For the former, it is about freedom, safety, and family and for the latter is about having money to care for her children.

Perhaps you are someone who believes abundance means having it all—plenty of wealth, good relationships, excellent health, and family. The reality is that you can have it all. Purposeful, focused, and magnetized thoughts and feelings bring whatever you desire.

195. Suspend Your Disbelief

You must suspend the disbelief that you can have wealth, even if you know your sneakers have holes in the soles and your present financial hardships are oppressive and seemingly unrelenting. You can think like the pessimist that wealth is not and can never be part of your life and your thoughts and feelings will make it so. Or, you can become the optimist and see yourself feeling the elation of acquiring, holding onto, and increasing the currency flowing into your life right now. It takes only a necessary shift in consciousness. Take that first big, bold step toward the money you desire to claim and the magic and power in that step forward can launch the process.

196. Never Use the Words Debt and Bill

Words like *debt* and *bill* are supercharged with negativity. If you try to formulate a positive affirmation such as, "I am happy that I'm getting out of debt" the subconscious will key in on the word *debt* and bring you more. Ditto for the word *bill*. It is far better to write out an affirmation that excludes those two words. For example, "I am happy that my money increases every day and that I can now pay off my car." Or, "I am overjoyed that my wealth is growing daily, and I can easily make my mortgage payment with plenty of money left over."

197. Remember that Money Is Not Everything

Beware of magnifying the importance of money so much that you begin to hoard it. Making money into your God will thwart your efforts in bringing more of it to you. Remember that money must circulate. As it comes, express gratitude and share or tithe a percentage to your church, favorite cause, or someone in need.

The universe is rich beyond the human mind's ability to grasp just how abundant it is. It is counterproductive to flip back and forth between the extremes of thoughts of being greedy or thoughts of having lack. Rather, cultivate a steady positive focus on joyful confidence that whatever you desire and intend to have is already on its way to you in this moment.

198. Think Like a Rockefeller

Wealth magnet John D. Rockefeller used to say that God gave him his money. Born in 1839 on a New York farm, Rockefeller was the second of six children born to William A. and Eliza Rockefeller. John's life was informed by his work ethic, family training, religious beliefs, and financial habits. Hearing a minister once say "Get money; get it honestly, and give it wisely," was a moment of epiphany for Rockefeller. Those words became the financial plan for his life.

After making his fortune as founder of the Standard Oil Company, he stepped down from the daily leadership of the company when he was fifty-seven. From that point on, he focused on giving away the bulk of his fortune in philanthropic efforts to do the most good for human welfare.

199. Cultivate Compassion and Generosity

Everyone has a little adversity in life. Follow your passion, aligned with the Law of Attraction. Let your affirmations reflect your trust in a higher power. For example, try the following affirmation, "I am happy to be guided by the infinite wisdom that upholds creation in all my monetary affairs. As a child of the Divine, I am grateful for the blessings of grace through which money flows easily into my life. Just as I am receiving an abundance of money flowing into me from sources both known and unknown, so do I give generously to others."

200. Make a Wealth Receptacle

1. Find and decorate a tray, urn, hatbox, coffee can, or some other receptacle in red and gold, colors that attract prosperity.

2. On a piece of paper, write out your declarations for wealth, making them clear and succinct and including the time frame for when you want your wealth to manifest.

3. Put the paper of your wealth desires into a red envelope and drop it into the box.

4. Place the box in the wealth sector of your home or office near a money tree plant and a small bubbling fountain or aquarium. Finally place a small lamp or other light source in that sector with a red bulb.

201. Use Common Sense

If you are endeavoring to attract prosperity, you should avoid spending money you don't have. Don't expect that you'll go to sleep at night and when you awake in the morning that your wallet will be miraculously full of hundred dollar bills. Do watch for the *means* of prosperity to suddenly start showing up in your life as job offers or business connections, alliances, and new opportunities. At first, they may seem like coincidences or synchronicity at work.

202. Notice How The Universe is Bringing Wealth to You

Allow for money to flow in, even if you don't expect it or never considered it coming from a particular source. Do pay attention. Record the proof of the Law of Attraction at work by noting in your journal, diary, or scheduling book whenever you find a penny, get a gift certificate you didn't expect, receive a free Starbucks card, notice a forgotten five dollar bill in the pocket of a jacket you picked up at a yard sale, or other sign that the law is at work in your life.

203. Follow Your Bliss

Avail yourself of the opportunities that feel right to you. Just imagine if J.K. Rowling had not allowed the inspiration for the adolescent whiz Harry Potter to lead her into telling a story about the world of magic? What if Ralph Lauren had not decided to take his tie designs and found his own company, Polo Fashions, in 1968? And what if Oprah had decided that she could never hold her own in the world of daytime television talk shows?

CHAPTER 12

Steps You Can Take . . .

to Enhance Your Relationships

204. First, Love Yourself

True love starts with self love. You must love and respect your-self in order to unconditionally give and receive true love. The choice of a mate necessarily requires a deep understanding of who you are and what you desire as well as what you don't want in a lifelong partnership. Otherwise, you may tumble into a romance based on physical attraction and chemistry and only after you have become emotionally invested do you discover fatal flaws in the relationship.

The Law of Attraction will bring excellent candidates for your life partner. You help it accomplish that by a thorough understand-ing of your personality, what drives your choices, and what are your most important core beliefs and values. Then, you must decide what you seek in others.

205. Recognize the Effects of Brain Chemistry

The three stages of romantic love include lust, attraction (over-idealizing and fantasizing about the other person), and attachment (where fantasy love is replaced by real love and commitment). Fall-ing in love, your brain becomes flooded by dopamine (stimulates blissful feelings), norepinephrine (produces heightened attention, excitability) and lower levels of serotonin (suppresses neural circuits involved in assessing others).

Brain chemistry changes depending on how long you have been in love. Blind attraction does not necessarily ensure a long and last-ing commitment. Relationships often end because one or both of the individuals in the relationship could not overcome some quality, habit, or trait of the other once their brain chemistry returned to normal and reality set in.

206. Probe Below the Surface of Who You Are

Psychologists say that emotionally healthy people who thrive in strong, committed relationships may have had the advantage of having healthy relationships modeled for them. Their interpersonal relationships include such elements as respect, boundaries, truthfulness, and transparency. Others, who seem to always attract losers may have had less nurturing models or are driven by psychological factors (such as the need to rescue, seek father figures, date "bad boys" or "divas" and "drama queens," choose losers because their own self-esteem is low, etc.).

207. Beware of Falling into Destructive Patterns

Do you keep attracting the same type of person, at first believing your new love to be the ideal romantic partner, only to discover that you are not good together? Are you are an incurable romantic who falls in love at first sight and all too soon has to accept the end of the relationship. Maybe you prefer romantic partners who remind you of someone in your past or in your family (father figure, for example). Do you seek people whose attitudes are compatible with yours but their personalities are not? Does it seem that you are always attracted to your mirror opposite?

208. Navigate Emotional/Cultural Minefields

Lack of trust, anger, and resentment soon replace the love and commitment you thought you both shared. If you had a different cultural upbringing, you also may have cultural as well as psychological minefields to navigate and that will require patience, understanding, and special communication skills. But as Mother Teresa once observed, love is a fruit always in season and within everyone's reach. A better understanding of your own core values, beliefs, and attitudes help you refine ideas about what you desire in an ideal mate.

209. Find Someone with a Similar Personality

When a couple can both give and receive unconditional love and respect, the relationship thrives. It suffers, however, in an atmosphere of deceit, an imbalance of power, unrevealed expectations, or betrayal. Psychologists say that the act of betrayal is often so damaging to the persons experiencing the betrayal, roughly one-third of them become clinically depressed. The key to finding that perfect mate lies in your deliberate work with the Law of Attraction to bring into your life someone whose personality is similar to yours.

210. Be the Kind of Partner You Want

Every moment in a relationship, you have the power to feel positive or negative, beautiful or not, full of hopes and dreams, or just hanging on. When you are with someone special and slip into patterns of fault finding, sarcasm, criticism, whining, or sniping, you are setting yourself up to elicit negative responses. Be the lover you want your partner to be. Remember that true love is taking care of the other person's happiness because it is essential to yours.

211. Create a Healthy Cycle

When you attract people who respect and care for you, it makes you feel good about yourself. They appreciate you, tell you, and demonstrate it. That, in turn, endears them to you and raises your self-esteem. You are inclined to return to them the love and attention they are showering upon you. Your praise and loving actions induces them to show more positive and romantic behavior. The cycle creates a healthy environment for your relationship to blossom.

There are proven ways to attract someone good. When you establish firm boundaries, you draw to you emotionally healthy people. When you demonstrate loyalty and trust, you attract those who honor commitments. Cultivating these qualities will support your work of attracting others for whom these things are important.

212. Watch Your Triggers

Each time you find yourself in a foul mood and ready to pick a fight with your partner, think back to the exact moment you first began to feel negative. What triggered the shift? Understanding the triggers can enable you to choose to respond differently. Past hurts can cause you to slip into knee-jerk reactions to something your partner says or does. Take responsibility for your role in the argument. If it's part of an old pattern, watch for the triggers and shift the energy.

213. Invite the Perfect Romantic Partner into Your Life

The Law of Attraction will bring someone perfect for you, if you allow for that to happen in your life. Focus on the life you want with the kind of person you want. Feel joy, gratitude, and peace to raise your vibration to draw that person to you. You have a choice in every moment to be available to love. Put your attention there and the attraction begins. Don't worry about when, where, or how it will happen. Know that someone special is en route to you at this moment. The speed of the arrival is directly related to the strength and magnetism of your thoughts, intention, and desire.

214. Contemplate the Qualities You Most Desire

Make a list of the good qualities you seek in a partner and why. If it makes it easier, list the qualities you don't want and then use each in a sentence that states the opposite, or the quality that you do want. For example: I feel insulted and disrespected when I hear profanity carelessly peppered throughout my date's vocabulary when around me (negative statement). I feel happy, loved, and respected when my date is thoughtful and considerate about word choices when around me (positive statement).

215. Turn the Light on for Love

An omnipresent spiritual force begins to draw into your life the love you desire at the moment you decide to open your heart and life to receive that special someone. You might run into that person while taking out the garbage . . . or on the subway . . . or at the bank. Look your best from the inside out. That means love yourself enough to take good care of you. That, in short, is how you turn on the switch for love. Physical, mental, and spiritual health generates the "light" of your inner being. Let it shine forth.

216. Make Space in Your Life for Love

Practice the art of loving another with understanding, patience, and insight. When you find someone new who might be the "one," take care to love that person as you desire to be loved in return. Take time to listen. Compliment him or her and be truthful and sincere. Remember to say thank you. Draw more love to you by affirming your love, showing love, speaking of love, and writing love poems or letters to the one you love.

217. Use Love to Turn Away Hostility

Love can be a powerful healing potion. When a friend or romantic partner is upset and directs anger and hostility toward you, find a way to defuse the anger but attempt to understand what is at the heart of the problem and why you are the target of the anger. Discuss the problem in language that is nonthreatening or accusatory. Show empathy and recognition of what she might be experiencing. Say, "I can see that you are feeling upset," or "You must feel terrible right now," or "I understand how deeply wounded you are feeling." The angry individual needs to know that you recognize the truth of her frustration, anger, or pain. Seeing your empathy, she may become calm and better able to coherently discuss the situation.

218. Avoid Passive-Aggressive People

Passive-aggressive behavior is not always easy to recognize or understand. The passive-aggressive person will dilly-dally around to avoid doing a task (even though he knows it is his responsibility). He will also avoid confrontation over not doing it and feel picked on when directly accused. He will get back at you indirectly and won't let you know why. Or, he will have a pattern of saying something mean to you and then add, ". . . just kidding." He's not. He may have a persistent pessimistic pattern of thinking.

When you set forth your desire to attract people into your life for interpersonal relationships, you will ask the universe for emotionally and psychologically healthy individuals.

219. Do Not Tolerate Abuse

Refuse to accept bad behaviors such as aggression, yelling, manipulation, deception, lies, threats, and intimidation. Recognize such actions for what they are—abusive behavior. Often such behaviors are byproducts of addictions or emotional issues and are destructive to a relationship. Set boundaries. If they are not honored, end the relationship to protect yourself.

If you are already in a committed relationship with someone who has anger issues or has passive-aggressive behaviors or if you have family members or friends with symptoms, take heart. You have myriad sources available to you to learn about how to deal with such behaviors. Read more at the National Institutes for Health at *www.nlm.nih.gov/*.

CHAPTER 13

Steps You Can Take . . .

to Strengthen Your Faith

220. Draw Spiritual Resources into Your Life

If you have deep spiritual convictions that you try to live by, but find it difficult to develop spiritually while juggling a career, family obligations, and other responsibilities, you are not alone. People in America are stressed out, get too little sleep, and have so many responsibilities that finding a way to squeeze out an extra hour now and then for meditation or other spiritual practices seems near impossible. But the Law of Attraction will bring you spiritual opportunities, teachers, helpers, and other resources you might need. And you may even see the boundaries blurring between the spiritual and physical worlds.

221. Follow Your Own Path

Whatever your spiritual philosophy, be assured that the Law of Attraction works alongside all belief systems. Whatever is at the top of the spiritual mountain, there are certainly myriad paths upward. Stick to what feels right to you and the law will bring you what you pray for, think about, or deeply desire from your belief system. It does not discriminate because it is drawing to you what your emotions and thoughts focus on. If you change your belief system and desire to align with a different spiritual path, the law is still working in tune with your thoughts. A person can be deeply spiritual and not be aligned with a particular religion and yet the law works with them just the same.

222. Always Think for Yourself

While atheists claim Einstein never believed in a personal God, others say he did and point to his famous statement, "God does not play dice," as proof. But Einstein, raised a secular Jew, abhorred having his spiritual beliefs misrepresented and stated that he did not believe in a personal God. He said that his was rather an admiration without limits for the "structure of the world" inasmuch as science reveals it. Einstein engaged in original thought. He did not let others do his thinking for him. Perhaps that resonates with your feeling about the universe and creation and spirituality.

223. Let Your Dharma be Your Guide

Dharma is a way of living in which the body, mind, and spirit are in perfect alignment. You must have faith that you can achieve your goals and dreams regardless of whether or not anyone else believes in what you want to do. When your life's work is not different than your spiritual work, you are following your dharma.

Your endeavors on the spiritual plane inform your thoughts and actions in the world and set into motion a creative force to help you achieve success in whatever you do. Wallace Wattles noted that when you desire to do something, the desire alone is the proof that the power you need to do that work is already inside you.

224. Answer the Call to a Spiritual Adventure

Perhaps you have dreamed about undertaking some fantastic spiritual adventure somewhere in the world, possibly to hike the sacred landscape of Machu Picchu in Peru, pray at the shrine of Mary Magdalene at Vezelay in France, trek the last twenty miles of the road to Santiago di Compostela in Spain, or see the caves of the ancient Anasazi in New Mexico. Don't let self-limiting thoughts about being too old, out of shape, or fear of being alone limit your experience. Remember Abraham, the Jewish patriarch, was seventy-five years old when he received a divine call to leave Ur to undertake a journey to Canaan, a strange and distant place.

225. Receive Divine Gifts with Gratitude

When you get the "call" to do something spiritual, don't let fear and old patterns of doubt and negative self-talk hold you back. Feel jubilant that you know from the deeps of your being what you are now supposed to do. You have received the gift, the inspiration…not someone else. Be grateful and make the most of it. Old Abraham might have wondered if he weren't just hatching some crazy plan in his daydreaming mind. Did he think about possible negative consequences of just pulling up the stakes of the tent and setting off toward that strange land? Nope, he heeded the call and felt blessed to be on his way.

226. Listen for Guidance from Within

What spiritually great things could you accomplish if you, like Abraham, believed that you were being guided, inspired, and blessed in all your endeavors by the greatest power in the universe and you had only to be quiet to receive direction? Abraham's clear inner vision and outer action were perfectly aligned. "Abram: I am thy shield, and thy exceeding great reward" (Genesis 15: 1). What tremendous power those words must have had for Abraham. The everlasting covenant between the God of Abraham and the Jewish people, through the rite of circumcision, endures to this day. In the history of the humankind, Abraham stands as a spiritual giant because he did not hesitate to follow the guidance he received.

227. Believe in the Force of Your Convictions

When you see something that you know is morally wrong, whatever your spiritual traditions and beliefs, do something, say something, be an advocate for right thinking and action. Hold tight to your convictions for they set up a pull for the Law of Attraction to draw to you other likeminded people who will help you in the cause. It's not always easy to know what to do when you see the tide of public opinion unopposed to something you feel is spiritually wrong.

---

228. Work Toward Social Justice

Do spiritual work with a single-minded focus and you will be following your true nature aligned with the Divine. That is dharma (a Sanskrit word that means "teaching, sustaining, supporting"). Effort in harmonious alignment with dharma will unify. A good example of a historical figure following his dharma is Mohandas Gandhi. He was simultaneously a spiritual giant and a diminutive man in a loin cloth who brought England to its knees and secured India's independence. His life serves as a spiritual model for social change.

229. Don't Be Discouraged by Your Circumstances

You don't have to hold degrees from the best schools, wear this season's haute couture, speak six languages, or serve in the diplomatic corps to be a spiritual force for social change. Gandhi began to study religion and eat a vegetarian diet while he trained as a lawyer in England. Unable to find work after returning to India, he went to South Africa where he encountered racism and social injustice. There, he successfully spearheaded nonviolent resistance to help Indians fight a law aimed at forcing them to register. Returning to India, he again used civil disobedience in the Quit India campaign to expel the English. Some called him a saint trying to be a politician, but Gandhi rejected that idea, insisting instead that he was a politician trying to become a saint.

230. Use Your Gifts to Help Others

If you think your spiritual work can only be done in private, think again. You don't have to go off to an isolated cave in the Himalayas. You don't have to join a Carmelite convent. You don't need to go outside of yourself to find spiritual understanding, insights, and peace.

Whatever your path, your efforts to deepen your spiritual experience, increase your knowledge, and raise your vibration can be done in all types of environments and conditions. Find your path. You'll know you are on it when you see how easily your thoughts, spiritual desires, and actions are aligned. These things synchronize your soul call with the great power of the Law of Attraction to manifest your spiritual gifts . . . gifts you can use for the greater social good.

231. Be Aware of Synchronicity

Many people have experienced coincidences in their lives, but when such events are multiple (two or more) and meaningful without any relationship in their causes, synchronicity is surely at work. You may not notice it, but synchronicity is going on all the time. Learn to live your life in a magical yet purposeful way, and you'll begin to see the meaningful (even mystical) occurrences in life that you may be missing because you are distracted or too busy or tired to notice. Synchronicities are those little meaningful coincidences that can point you in new directions or provide you with moments of breakthrough understanding. The more you notice them, the more of them, seemingly, there are to notice.

232. Observe the Patterns that Reveal Themselves

Swiss psychologist Carl Gustav Jung coined the term "synchronicity." Jung offered psychological insights into human consciousness as a result of viewing the psyche through the lenses of myth, art, religion, philosophy, and dreams. Jung's interest in Eastern religions and philosophies after traveling to India influenced and informed his ideas about the importance of the unconscious and value of daily spiritual practice.

Synchronicity is one indicator that the Law of Attraction is at work and that something you have asked for is beginning to make its way to you. It bears repeating that it is worthwhile to pay attention to coincidences. Watch for evidence of meaningful occurrences and their connectivity. Notice patterns of flow, when things easily happen or come together. Observe how little signs begin to show up and give notice that Universe has received your request.

233. Achieve Spiritual Results

Maybe you desire to dive deeper in meditation than you have ever gone. Perhaps you want to replace a bad habit with a good one that better serves your spiritual endeavors. Maybe you seek inspiration for meaningful spiritual work you can do to benefit the world. Or you seek a teacher or inspiration for the direction to take on your personal spiritual path. You can do all those things and even more by deliberate and intentional work with the Law of Attraction.

234. Keep in Mind How the Law Works

The Law of Attraction works whether you nurture the Divine within and seek increase for your spiritual life or if you do things that evoke the law of decrease. When you criticize others, demean a person's choices, devalue someone's work, or spread gossip about someone, you are setting in motion three universal laws: the Law of Decrease, the Law of Karma, and the Law of Attraction. Don't waste your mental currency on such negative activity since it will return to you in kind. Instead, focus on working with the Law of Increase and the Law of Attraction to manifest spiritual results.

235. Manifest Whatever You Desire

The ego is what creates the sense of your separation from the Divine. In meditation, the ego's hold can lessen as you transcend into higher states of consciousness. Deepak Chopra writes in his book, *The Seven Spiritual Laws of Success*, all things are possible within the realm of pure consciousness, and that pure consciousness is your essential nature. You experience the truth of who you really are—a spark of the eternal One in the energy field of pure potentiality. In that realm of knowing, you can manifest anything.

236. Detach Yourself from Doubt

Knowing that you can create any dream from the field of infinite potentiality, you can let go of attachment to the outcome. The notion of detachment may be for some a little more difficult concept to grasp. It requires letting go of the attachment to the result. That doesn't mean you have to let go of your intention to manifest something. To be able to detach from an outcome means that you have a deep abiding conviction in your true Self's power to create anything you need, want, or desire.

237. Meditate for Solutions to Your Problems

Regular daily meditation, even though the time may be only ten minutes or so, offers a period of relief from life's constant barrage of stimulation and problems. When you meditate, you temporarily shut off the senses, calm your breathing, and allow your brain to rest and recharge. Then, an amazing thing happens. After a period of inner stillness when you again bring mental focus upon a problem, solutions may pop into your mind. Such options may be ones you never thought of because your hyperfocus on the problem blocked them.

238. Shift Your Vibration to Find Answers

You can also bring about an energy shift by doing something physical. Leave your problem at the house or office and take a walk in nature. The energy vibration of nature can calm you. Not thinking about the problem while you enjoy a stroll around a lake, through the woods, on the beach, around a park, or across a meadow clears and refreshes your mind. The Law of Attraction, as you know, is always at work. When you detach from the problems, knowing with deep conviction that inherent in every problem is the means to solve it, the law can effortlessly deliver a solution . . . and sometimes surprising ones.

239. Enhance Your Life by Attracting What You Want

The Law of Attraction responds to emotional shifts up and down. Depression, anger, sadness are stark contrasts to joy, love, and happiness. Dark feelings function as radar. They signal that your thoughts have turned negative. To return to a positive mood and thus a higher vibration, you have to shift your thoughts until your feelings begin to shift.

Your power to shift emotion up and down by your thoughts means you can live your life from the inside out with the knowledge of how to deliberately attract the good things in life. You'll have greater satisfaction as you work your own thoughts and emotions to directly experience your true self and divine purpose in life (dharma). Finally, you will have the knowledge and experience to work with the universal laws to create virtually anything.

CHAPTER 14

Steps Your Can Take . . .

to Manifest Success in Your Career

240. Identify Your Core Values

Your success in business happens in alignment with your core values and your business beliefs and practices. Business is about relationships. You have already assessed your core values as they pertain to relationships. It would be wise to also know your values and beliefs as they pertain to your relationships in the business world.

There are many reasons why you may not be manifesting success on your chosen career track, with your job, your small business, or other areas pertaining to work. One possibility could be a conflict between your core values and those of the company that employs you or other companies with whom you must conduct business. Perhaps you are expected to do something that is at cross-purposes with your ethics.

241. Create a Mission Statement

Many business professionals understand that a dynamic work environment that nurtures the creative spirit plays an important role in the success of workers and the company. Companies usually state their core values in their mission statements. Disney has perhaps the shortest mission statement ever. It succinctly states its goal is to make people happy.

A mission statement tells your customers, community, workers, suppliers, and funding people what your business is about. It succinctly states enterprise's purpose, intention, and guiding principles and core values. A mission statement is sometimes combined with a vision statement focusing on future goals.

242. Find Ways to Thrive Where You Are

If you are employed with a company in a job does not feel right, but you need the paycheck and have no good options for moving, consider working with the Law of Attraction to inspire and guide you to a new position in your current company. Until you can locate another potential place of employment, you have to think of what to do from where you currently are. It may mean staying in the dead-end job until exit is possible. Don't be disheartened. Plant the seeds of desire and intent today so that the universe can rearrange itself to give you that new job.

243. Know Where You Are Going

Remember the words of the Cheshire Cat in Lewis Carroll's *Alice in Wonderland*, "If you don't know where you are going, it doesn't matter which way you go." When you know what you desire and where you intend to head and for what purpose, the paradigm shifts and sets into motion a new reality for you.

Be on the lookout for great, new ideas. You don't have to be first at something, but endeavor to be the best. If you are the person in charge of your company, hire excellent workers who are quick at executing orders. Create incentives to inspire employees to be innovative, organized, efficient, and forward-thinking and do impeccable work, maintain quality, and stick to deadlines.

244. Visualize Your Ideal Job

Begin thinking about your dream job and how passionate you feel doing it. If that job doesn't exist, don't give up. Create that ideal job by impressing your thoughts and your dreams upon what Wallace D. Wattles calls the "formless substance." Simply see it in your mind. In the energy field of the all-pervasive spirit, all things are related through interconnectedness. When you change, the universe changes, too. Some of the most creative people in the world have imagined totally new jobs and careers that didn't exist.

245. Be as Specific as Possible

Envision everything associated with your ideal job. Tailor your desires. Be specific. Refine. Just the thought of being able to achieve your goals increases clarity and determination. What type of work is it? What tasks are you required to do? What does the office building look like? Who are the other workers (for example, are they highly skilled international workers or highly diverse mostly college-age whiz kids)? What are the work hours/schedule? How much money do you make? What is your title? Can you see yourself owning the company?

246. Cultivate Determination and Persistent Desire

If you want success and financial prosperity in the business/work area of your life, then you must hang on tenaciously to your dream and deeply focus your intention on having it. Know that you are not living in a zero sum universe. When abundance comes to you, that does not mean it leaves someone else. See your work as increasing the good in the lives of your coworkers and customers. Believe that your business transactions enrich the lives of others and never subtract from them.

247. Use the Powerful Tool of Intuition

Regardless of what you call it—intuition, sixth sense, instinct—everyone has the ability to some degree to sense things. By practicing relaxation and calming of the mind, you clear out the mental clutter and quiet the chattering to allow for intuition to bring forth innovative ideas, solutions, and concepts to help you meet professional business goals and get results.

Donald Trump relies on his instincts in business and is also guided by a few principles: discipline, honesty, hard work, responsiveness to others, flexibility, and reliance and trust of a core group of talented, smart people.

248. Remember the Value of Gratitude

The creative force of the universe responds to expressions of gratitude. When you feel and express your appreciation for the good things that have manifested in your life, an attraction is established with infinite potential to bring more goodness. When you inform your friends of your desire to find a new job, for example, and then they start bringing you notices of employment opportunities, praise their efforts. After your interviews with prospective employers, say thank you and send a follow-up card expressing your appreciation.

249. Always Think of Others

Consider how your business decisions positively impact others in your business environment and your community. The recent scare over lead paint in toys imported from China is an example of how a business and its leaders impact others, in that case, the end user—children and their families. Another example is paying lower than cost-of living wages to unskilled workers. Aim for the moral high ground. There is nothing wrong with always trying to do the right thing.

When you have a business problem, try to solve it so that all involved parties benefit by the solution. Get involved in outreach programs on behalf of your business to help others. Become a socially responsible citizen. As you seek the highest good for all concerned, increased goodness returns to you in myriad ways.

250. Be a Team Player

Perhaps you have carefully orchestrated your climb to the top and have taken on more and more responsibility along the way. In the final analysis, you, and every other worker, are always going to be judged on the quality of the work done. If your organization is one in which the structure emphasizes a team approach rather than dazzling solo acts, you will want to be a team player. The quality of the team's work will be more important than any individual's. Teachers of the Law of Attraction suggest that you, possibly with others, have created the reality in which competition drives the outcome of winner and loser. If your single-minded attention had been to achieve that specific goal, you'd have done it . . . but your intention was to *compete* for that goal.

251. Change the Rules

You, perhaps with coworkers or others, created a reality that dictated a winner and loser. You may have the intention to win, but the rules you created make it also possible for you to lose. Change the rules and you set up a different environment for the outcome, that is, maybe you don't win at the top, but win in some way on some level. Here's an example of the same idea using others in the company. Instead of celebrating the achievement of only your top salesperson, establish several levels of winners. In that way, one person's gain (in this case, the top seller) won't dictate that everyone else necessarily loses (all the other salespeople). High achievers are rewarded, others are acknowledged for their hard work, and no one gets left out.

252. Manifest the Raise You Deserve

The secret to working with the Law of Attraction to manifest the perfect job, raise, or promotion is to create a powerful, compelling mental video that excites you every time you play it forward in your mind. To get the raise you want, see yourself meeting with the person empowered to grant the raise. Think, act, and speak during the meeting as if the raise has already been approved. Feel the elation of knowing that your next paycheck will include that money. Imagine how you will use it. Use affirmations, visualizations, journal writing, and poster-making projects to intentionally reprogram your thoughts to accept that you have been given the raise.

253. Earn a Promotion or Attain Your Dream Job

See yourself in your mental video receiving the news that your promotion has come through. See yourself at a company meeting where your promotion is announced. Now play the video forward to hear the high praises your boss shares about you and your work with others attending your celebration party. Feel all the positive feelings associated with being in your new elevated position.

For the mental video of your dream job, see yourself already in that job. Take a look at the business card you are holding with your name on it. Feel the pleasure of seeing your name and position. Hand your card to someone influential in the sphere of your chosen field of work or a venture capitalist. See yourself easily discussing your mission statement with that person.

254. Affirm Your Way to Career Success

Try the following affirmation for finding the perfect new job. "I am elated to know that the Law of Attraction is in the process of guiding me to a new job where I can best express my skills and talents and where my salary increases and my coworkers and bosses appreciate my contributions." Now you try to write your own affirmation by filling in the blanks. "I feel _____(name a positive emotion) to know that the job of _____(name the job or insert "my perfect job") is in the process of manifesting in my life right now.

255. Use Optimism to Grow Your Business

Perhaps you are self-employed and love your work but would like to see the company grow and become more profitable. You can hasten the arrival of that desire by raising your vibration with optimism and hope and opening your heart to allow for the dream to manifest. Let go of self-limiting beliefs and doubts. You need to create and hold in your mind a clear, new vision for your company. When you are passionate about your endeavors and do the best you are capable of doing, the fruit of the labor (increased business, profits, expanded contacts, more clients and customers, etc.) naturally unfolds according to the law.

256. Create the Master Plan in Your Mind

Write your vision as a declaration of desire or mission statement. Turn the vision into images you put on a poster. Find a symbol that represents everything you want the company to become. Use that symbol as a touchstone throughout the day to remember to visualize, affirm, feel the emotion of succeeding, and know that everything you have created in your vision is in the processes of manifesting. Napoleon Hill counseled that to receive that which you desire to manifest, you first have to believe it is possible that you can acquire it.

257. Treat Others with Respect

In the world of business, people have different styles of working together or managing and leading others. Some are confrontational while others are consensus builders or transformational. Treat everyone—from the lowest-level position in the company to managers and even the millionaire investor advising you—with the same respect and appreciation for contributions to your business. Negative emotion does not place you in harmonious alignment with the Law of Attraction, but positive, respectful and visionary energy does. See everyone as deserving of riches, success, prosperity, and recognition of achievements.

258. Make Lists of Specific Tasks and Responsibilities

You believe that you are ready for fast track advancement to the top of your company or career. Or, you desire to start your own business. Remember that what you focus on, you attract. Make a list of all the things you want in terms of advancement. For example, your list could include more task-related items such as more and varied responsibilities, opportunities for the most challenging assignments, a senior level management or higher position, and greater autonomy to do your job as well as rewards and perks such as performance bonuses, increased industry recognition, a company car, and international travel.

259. Shift Your Mind Away from Worry

Stop worrying about how things will happen. Aim your mental laser beam on what you want. You will find that your intuition or instincts begin to guide you to opportunities for rapid advancement. Most importantly, the movement will occur effortlessly and easily.

So, if you want to create something, like shifting a negative attitude to a positive one, it can happen instantly because your consciousness is timeless or eternal. The following negative thought, "I resent how my boss works with me under pressure because that frenetic energy causes me to feel stressful" can instantly become "I am grateful for how my boss mentors me because learning from her helps me to advance rapidly within the company." It's always a good idea to de-emphasize the negative and focus on the positive.

260. Seek Success from the Inside Out

To be successful in the world, you have to feel successful. There are plenty of people who seem to have everything—money, family, friends, beautiful children, an affluent lifestyle, great job—and yet satisfaction with life eludes them. They may have addiction problems because of the excesses of their lifestyles or legal problems or tax issues. Trouble follows them like a dog nipping at their heels no matter where they go and what they do. They chase success and never find it.

Cultivate your belief in yourself as a successful person. What does your success look like? Wealth, health, great relationships, fabulous job—whatever it is, play the mental video of it over and over again. Think and feel successful. Don't let anything or anyone dim that vision.

261. Stay Positive and Success Will Follow

Believe that you deserve the best. Enjoy getting it. When you are on track in your job, business, or career, you exude happiness. Joy fills every fiber of your being when you are engaged in doing what you love and though you may do it repeatedly, you still look forward to that activity. Absorbed in doing work for its own the sake, you lose your sense of time while the creative force of the cosmos flows through you.

Whatever type of work you are involved in, do it well. Earn as much money as you honorably can and, as you are able, give some to others. Strive for excellence and live by noble principles and values. Stay positive and optimistic and know the Law of Attraction is working with you.

Steps You Can Take . . .

to Find Enlightenment in Music and Art

262. Become More Deeply Focused

Use music and art to redirect patterns of negative thought into positive channels to shift your consciousness. Not only does music help raise your mood and thus your vibration, the right choice of music can establish a conducive atmosphere for prayers or a meditation and relaxation session. It can also diffuse undesirable energies of others around you.

Listen to quiet uplifting music when reciting mantras or prayers on your japa mala (a string of prayer beads, usually numbering one hundred and eight beads) or a rosary. Strive to stay in harmonious alignment with the Law of Attraction to effect change in your life and for the greater good. Use music to dive more deeply into everything you do.

263. Elevate Your Mood

Music plays an integral role in gratitude. As you have learned, expression of gratitude is a major key to living an abundant life. Listening to a beautiful piece of music inspires reverence and appreciation for the gifts of the Divine and the grandeur and wonder of life.

To reach the deepest levels of spiritual consciousness and super wisdom is akin to peeling away layers of ignorance like the skin of an onion until you reach the heart. Music can take you down into deeper layers. One way to penetrate those layers is to use music that you like to elevate your mood. When you are feeling positive you are most likely able to also feel gratitude for your spiritual gifts, especially on days when they seem to be not gifts but burdens.

264. Tune Your Chakra Vibrational Makeup

Chakras or the force centers of the ethereal body respond to sound vibrations. Some musicians and yogis say that chakra tuning and healings can be brought about through the use of sound. Also, your chakras, according to some metaphysical schools of thought, have an energetic vibration associated to psychological well-being. The right music can help you function at optimum levels.

Music has been hailed a powerful tool in healing. Some say it works at the cellular level. The key to gain maximum benefit from music is to listen attentively and then mentally check in to see how you feel. If it makes you feel good, then use it often to raise your vibration in order to be in harmonious alignment with the Law of Attraction.

265. Receive Healing through Art and Music Therapy

Art and music are often combined in therapy sessions aimed at helping you work through psychological pain and emotional trauma. In a safe environment provided by a therapist or health professional, you may be encouraged to listen to the soothing cross-species sounds of nature, perhaps set to strains of classical music such as Pachelbel's "Canon in D" or Barber's "Adagio for Strings."

If you are feeling stuck or emotionally pulled in different directions, express your innermost feelings by playing music or creating art. Working through grief, illness, abuse, or deep psychological wounds enables you to finally release the energy associated with holding onto that pain. Breakthroughs of insight or understanding are also possible. With release, damaging stress levels dissipate and healing is facilitated. The goal is to restore emotional well-being and positive feelings.

266. Tune into the Mother of All Sounds

Follow the sound current of Aum (the cosmic vibration of atoms in creation) inward and your absorption into that Nada or Mother of All Sounds can take you to a state of *samadhi,* or at-oneness with the Divine. The most powerful place in meditation is the space between thoughts. For however long you can experience the absence of thought, dive deeply inward, toward the Source of your being.

In Shabda practice, you concentrate on not only sound but also meaning and vibration. Of the three, the sages say that vibration is the most important because when you tune in to the vibration of Aum, in which all sound is contained, you are aligning with those holy ones from ages past who have spiritually worked with the sound. Aum is an expression of the Divine.

267. Heighten Your Intention with Music

Ever wonder why you can put together a jigsaw puzzle more quickly if you do it while listening to music? Listening to music prepares your brain to do spatial tasks, but the effect is short lived because the improvement in your ability to solve spatial problems lasts only a short time after the music ends. The "opening" of the neural pathways may respond best to strains of classical music, which is more complex than other types of music. If your most burning desire is to create a masterful piece of art or composition, try listing to music to begin the Law of Attraction's pulling power. With focus and intent and a heightened sense of expectation, your masterpiece will emerge from within you.

268. **Play Music for Your Children**

Babies have billions of brain cells. Exposing them to classical music such as Mozart or Bach can foster a life-long love of music and facilitate the work of their brains to forge connections between patterns, language, and rhythms. As your children grow, consider securing for them a course of musical training and allowing them to learn to play a musical instrument to facilitate a deep and abiding attraction for music in their lives.

By listening to complex music compositions, your brain becomes primed to open pathways for solving spatial problems, forge connections that may make learning new subjects easier, and enhance positive mood. Such "improvement" in brain functioning enables clarification of intention and raises your vibration for working with the Law of Attraction.

269. **Stimulate those Young Brains**

Studies have shown a linkage between the ability to play music and to more easily solve spatial tasks, learn more quickly, and stimulate the brain in positive ways. Some studies suggest that babies as young as three months can recognize pieces of classical music which they have listened to in the past. Exposure to music can foster in them a lifelong music appreciation. And a love of music can help young adults begin to realize their dreams.

270. Access Whole Brain Functioning

Music is said to be the mechanism to cause new neural pathways to link the left and right hemispheres of the brain enabling, what scientists call, whole brain functioning. Music, some have said, is the language of the soul. While some individuals seeking to enter higher states of consciousness for healing, decision making, and creative endeavors might respond best to repetitive musical notes and words as might be found in the chanting of a mantra such as *Deva Premal Sings the Moola Mantra* (see *www.whiteswanrecords.com*) others might prefer the hot licks and backbeats of rhythm and blues or rock music.

271. Create a Dream-Fulfilling Work of Art

Let music give pleasure to your heart and the words of great beings inspire your thoughts as you begin to work manifesting. Use touchstones such as fetishes, symbols or icons, and words with special meaning to prepare you for your undertaking. The Taoist sage Lao Tzu asserted that "When you realize that there is nothing lacking, the whole world belongs to you." He also pointed out that "to the mind that is still, the entire universe surrenders."

In the stillness of peace, declare your intention to seek something from the universe or to give your own gifts to the world. Maybe you want to create a CD of spiritual music, a piece of visionary art, a self-help book, or whatever your dream is—create a collage or painting that depicts it.

272. Let Art and Music Guide You

Maybe your desire has not yet come into clear focus. Be patient and continue thinking about it. Lao Tzu also said that "at the center of your being, you have the answer; you." Let your subconscious guide you to powerful images. Clip them from magazines to use on a collage. As you listen to the strains of your favorite music, remember that in the ancient world, music was integrated into society in almost every conceivable way, from stick-banging in fields to frighten away birds (later accompanied by song) to the prayers offering religious sacrifices, and the celebration of battle victories. Let music lead you to the art that represents the new life or good world you are creating.

273. Follow the Pull of Your Subconscious

When you are making a collage by first cutting out images from a magazine, your conscious mind may choose many of the pictures or words, but something else may be taking place. You may be strongly attracted to a particular image without any idea of why. Definitely clip that image, too, because the reason you are drawn to it is found in your subconscious mind. It just might represent a long-suppressed desire that you would have manifested long ago if 1) you hadn't gone to medical school, 2) you never had enough money, 3) you had gotten married and had kids, 4) you bought a house, or a host of other reasons that may no longer have relevance. Pay attention to the things that capture your attention. What are they telling you about unfulfilled dreams or self worth?

274. Make Giving Thanks Part of Every Day

Let sound bring you peace, exhilaration, excitement, contentment, and happiness. Use sound to guide your thoughts and feelings to creating declarations of gratitude throughout your day. Make them part of a daily devotional walk or recite them as you prepare a meal for your family or friends that you want to infuse with love.

As you make known to the universe your desire to have increased confidence, heightened self-esteem, increased weight loss, a profitable new business, the perfect mate, a baby, or a thousand other things, remember to not only be thankful for the things you currently have but to use your feelings and thoughts to express your gratitude.

275. Use Your Most Powerful Tool

Gratitude has called by some experts of the Law of Attraction as the most powerful tool at your disposal to aid in manifesting your goals, dreams, and desires. You can certainly use music, art, affirmations, visualizations, journaling, dream incubations, and other modalities to establish an attraction for the things you want in your life, but you hasten the work of the law when your thoughts, feelings, and actions are harmoniously aligned in an attitude of gratitude.

276. Open Your Heart to Help Others

Use music and art to gain greater understanding into the human condition and perhaps do something about the plight of others less fortunate. Kindred spirits who believe that human civilization has evolved to a place of potential destruction share a common desire for social transformation and are using music, writing, discourse, and art to shift old paradigms.

Consider using what you've learned in the journey of life and your deliberate work with the Law of Attraction to make the world a better place. By opening your heart to help others, you are making a channel for the Law of Attraction to bring good things and the love of others to you.

277. Let Love Flow

Love, some say, is itself a vibration. Left unimpeded, love can flow easily between humans. But when love meets resistance in the form of deep-seated selfishness, fear, angst, and a need to control, its flow becomes as impeded or erratic as surely as when a stream hits a narrow gorge or tumbles onto a craggy beach filled with boulders. When you block giving or receiving love, you are thwarting your opportunity to be nourished as intended by the heart of the Divine.

278. Call Upon Kindred Spirits on Your Journey

Just as people band together to effect social change, work for political goals, or to collectively hold a new vision for the world, people can be attracted into your life to help you achieve success. Such individuals include teachers, community leaders, clergy people, business advisors, financial planners, Feng Shui experts, personal coaches, psychologists, musicians and artists, or those belonging to a support network who have been through some life experience that you currently find challenging.

279. Listen to Your Intuition

Do you place more value on your rational thinking than your intuitive thoughts? Perhaps you should re-think that. A well-known and oft-recited quote by Einstein is, "I never came upon any of my discoveries through the process of rational thinking." Noting that gift of an intuitive mind was the only thing of true value, Einstein also believed that the spirit manifested in the harmonies of the universe best represented the God in whom he deeply believed.

280. Use Music to Develop Your Psychic Talent

Draw upon music to induce a relaxed state in which you rely less upon rational thinking and more upon intuition and inner guidance. Clear your mental clutter. Open yourself to information accessible from realms other than that of the material/physical and be willing to doubt the current thinking about something in order to entertain new ideas about it.

Some people believe strongly that angels and nature spirits are around each person and available for help as you travel on the journey through your life. Generally, you seek such help through intuition. You may also benefit from learning to bring forth intuitive thoughts through automatic writing, pendulum dowsing, and deciphering information from Tarot cards, the *I Ching*, and scrying (interpreting images/messages revealed in a bowl of water or a crystal ball).

CHAPTER 16

Steps You Can Take . . .

to Create Harmony in Your Home

281. Try Feng Shui

If the Law of Attraction isn't working as well as you'd like, try empowering your attracting factors through Feng Shui. The heart and soul of Feng Shui, the ancient Chinese art of placement and arrangement, is the energy called chi, qi, or prana that permeates everything in the universe. A Feng Shui belief states that all of creation is made up of that energy vibrating at various frequencies and the flow of that energy impedes or enhances attracting power. Some assert that Feng Shui doubles the power of the Law of Attraction.

282. Get Stagnant Energy Flowing

You influence the flow of the life-affirming chi throughout your surroundings by the way you incorporate physical objects and plants in the interior as well as by your color choices, furniture and art placement, interior lighting, art objects, and symbolic items representing nature.

Take stock of your home to ascertain whether clutter blocks easy navigation through the entry and all areas of the house. Is the home painted and furnished in a way that creates a warm welcome? Has your collection taken over one or more areas of the house? Has your love of furniture overfilled rooms so that they feel crowded and cramped?

283. Open Up Your Living Space

In houses staged for sale, furniture is positioned in such a way as to allow potential buyers to see seventy percent of walls and floors because people who are in the market for a house want to see walls, ceilings, floors, and windows—not the items in the home. Likewise, in Feng Shui, floors and walls should be somewhat open to allow the free flowing of life-affirming chi.

When rooms are stuffed, the flow of energy is blocked and can become stagnant. Your goal is to ensure that there are open pathways through your home to allow the energy passage. When the energy can freely swirl around your environment (and by Feng Shui association, every area of your life), your good fortune or luck changes along with your power to intentionally attract what you desire.

284. Choose Furniture and Lighting Carefully

Furniture needs to not only support you but also give you enough of a feeling of safety and the security to express yourself. It shouldn't be too large or too small but rather be of a proper scale for the space. In group seating in living rooms, for example, furniture should offer options for differently sized people. The space should appear welcoming to all—an invitation to come, sit, and enjoy one another's company.

Living spaces need adequate illumination through the use of ambient lighting, spot lights, overhead lights, torchier lights, sconces, and candles. The most important source of illumination, however, is natural light. Even on dark, wintry days, throw open the curtains to let natural light flood the rooms of your home. The light's positive energy brings with it the healing chi of nature.

285. Bring Nature Indoors with Mirrors

Use a mirror positioned toward a window to reflect nature into a room and also make a room seem larger. For example, a room on the sixth floor of a beachfront condo might not provide a direct ocean view until a floor-to-ceiling, wall length mirror is positioned on the wall adjacent to the sliding glass doors. Suddenly, the ocean and sky along with magnificent sunsets and starry nights, previously seen looking at an angle through the glass doors, now are reflected in the mirror.

286. Group Art in Threes

When you add candles, books, art pieces, and chairs in groups of three, you keep the energy expansive. A single candle, solitary book, and only one chair in the space would appear parsimonious and contract the energy. Stagnant or blocked energy is created when you leave a solitary dead plant in the room, random boxes or piles of stuff that you haven't gotten around to organizing, or dark corners where you have failed to illuminate. Luckily, the ancient Chinese figured out "cures" for Feng Shui problems, a subject to be explored a little further into this chapter.

287. Improve the Flow of Energy

There are several ways to improve energy flow and establish a balance of masculine and feminine elements (yin/yang). For example, you could add some healthy plants, a judicious splash of contrast color, things to represent nature, and some good illumination and the chi flows easily. You will know that the chi is moving through that space because you will feel happy, harmonious, healthy, calm, peaceful, and relaxed. Those positive feelings associated with flowing chi are exactly the positive feelings that aid the work of the Law of Attraction if bestowing abundance in your life.

288. Match the Space to its Function

The point of Feng Shui is to create an energetically balanced space that supports you and your life choices, that invites you, friends, and family members into a sense of community. The interior space in which Feng Shui is properly utilized fosters the flow of energy that is correct for the function of that space. In a bedroom, the energy will be grounded and safe, harmonious and peaceful. A living room, on the other hand, might have more lively energy flowing through it. The energy in that space encourages acceptance, love, safety, and grounding, but with a smidgeon of risk as represented by the use of a splash of vibrant color, an object precariously placed, or a piece of visual art depicting something wildly imaginative as depicted in bold line and color.

289. Eliminate Clutter

Clutter suppresses and even obstructs energy flow. Stagnant or blocked energy or chi makes your life difficult. Sapped of energy, your health suffers. Stagnant energy also blocks the flow of money. It impedes the manifestation of healthy relationships. It obstructs advancements in your chosen career path. It can bring on depression and negative patterns of thought.

Organize a particular area of your home or office. Once that room or area is completed, tackle the next room and the next until the whole house is re-energized. Baskets (symbolizing the reeds and grasses of nature) with lids are great for organizing objects that were carried in and forgotten in a room. Left to pile up, they begin slow down or block the natural flow of energizing chi.

290. Balance Your Home to Improve Your Health

Have piles of books been there so long that you had forgotten about them and don't even see them when you enter the room? Are there piles of books, dead or dying plants, a couch, chair, or table with loose screws or broken legs? Since these things represent bad Feng Shui, there's a pretty good chance your health is being affected. Have you noticed feeling fatigued, drained, stressed, or unhappy? Such symptoms indicate an imbalance in the energy of your home.

To fix that room, remove any items broken or damaged. Take away or organize and store objects of clutter. Bring in fresh flowers, aesthetically pleasing pictures, and objects of art in the healing colors of nature. Add an accent in the color of green (earth) and gold (sun), two powerful elements of nature that are both necessary for a healthy life-giving energy.

291. Learn the Principles of Feng Shui

Use knowledge of Feng Shui to aid the work of the Law of Attraction to bring you robust health, increased stamina, enthusiastic energy, emotional and mental acuity, and exceptional dexterity and flexibility. Learn to balance the accumulation and release, the ancient yin/yang energies. Incorporate elements of nature and add Feng Shui cures to problem areas. Transform your life through the use of those principles and you will be establishing excellent Feng Shui. Your life will begin to change according to your new, more harmonious alignment with the Law of Attraction.

292. Understand Yin/Yang Energies

Yin and yang energy together make up chi. Yin and yang forms of energy are opposites of each other, just as the earth is opposite the sky, heads is the opposite of tails (on a coin), and matter is opposite energy. Each needs the other for completeness or wholeness, yet too much or too little of either creates imbalance. Think of yin as inert, matter, earth, quiet, reflective, dark, female, shadow, cold, valleys, moon, and grounded while yang is active, energetic, sky, boisterous, creative, light, male, sunbeams, hot, mountains, sun, and upward moving, as if toward the heavens.

293. Work with the Elements

The art of Feng Shui in home environments relies on incorporating five key elements found in nature—earth, metal, water, wood, and fire. Earth energy is that which is close to the ground: floor cushions, a low coffee table, and pine cones in a basket or a pottery bowl on the fireplace hearth.

Metal energy is found in rooms with minimalist furniture, white or monochromatic color schemes, lots of space, and order everywhere. Water is found in fountains, plants like ivy or baby's tears that cascade, and circular or organic shapes in furniture and art objects. You will find wood energy in bamboo poles or wood columns, candlesticks, and objects that have vertical height. Fire energy is represented by the color red, candles, fireplaces, and wood-burning stoves.

294. Look for Feng Shui Problems

You may need to do a little detective work to locate the Feng Shui problems or blockages in your home. You may not immediately know you have a problem. Or, you may observe some signs and symptoms that an imbalance exists but don't know where. For example, are you too tired to make love to your spouse? Check out your bedroom for chipped, broken, or otherwise damaged furniture or problematic mattress and box springs. These things, if broken or damaged, need to be fixed pronto to prevent your marital relationship from undergoing stresses that might cause it to completely break down.

295. Create Serenity in Your Bedroom

A bedroom needs to be suitable for sleeping—no piles of clothes on the side of the bed or clutter since the latter represents emotional junk, something you definitely don't want in the bedroom. Think of your bedroom as the most sacred of all the spaces in your home environment.

Surround yourself with colors on the walls and bed linens that are serene and peaceful. No wild and jazzy patterns. Ensure that the outside light flows easily through clean, washed windows and opened curtains. Make certain that art is tasteful and serene, even holy since your bedroom is the place where you leave behind the daily cares and worries to cross the threshold of the dreaming mind into the subconscious.

296. Rearrange Things to Re-Energize the Space

If you no longer have an attachment for a room or anything in it, it may be time to totally change things around to replenish or create new pathways for the flow of chi. Or, if you just want a little lift of the energy, bring in a table-top fountain, build a comfortable window seat with a view outside, or install a new kitchen island with space to hold cookbooks and a counter to sit and sip tea while staring outside into nature. Incorporate the five elements of nature in some way in that room to either soften or reinvigorate it.

297. Hang Wind Chimes for Increased Energy

In a room where the energy seems weak, bring in sound in the form of music with more high notes than low. A wind chime with high-pitched bells or cylinders will give you more energy than ones with low sounds. Tibetan bells are the best of all, because they are often harmonically tuned. Your mood will become more positive with every breeze that moves the bells. Another way to shift energy for a more positive mood is to put on a CD of Feng Shui music and do some yoga or breath work.

Steps You Can Take . . .

to Know If You Are On Track

298. Consider Dowsing for Answers

Pendulum dowsing has been around for thousands of years but recently has been used by some as a divining tool in conjunction with the Law of Attraction to determine if they are on the right track for drawing in the things they want. The pendulum can give yes/no answers. One of the earliest dowsing images carbon dates to circa 6000 B.C. Found in the Tassilin-Ajjer Mountains of eastern Algeria, it shows a human figure holding a forked stick. Ancient Egyptian and Chinese images of dowsing also have been discovered on shards on pottery and papyri.

299. Prepare to Dowse

Dress in comfortable clothes and sit in a softly lit area where there are fresh flowers, a glass of water, and peaceful instrumental music. Breathe deeply to release any tension remaining in the body. Once you are fully relaxed, offer a prayer to the Divine. Ring a sacred bell to summon your guardian angel or guide(s) who are bearers of light and knowledge. Tell them that you have questions for them, that you seek only truth, and that you appreciate their help. Offer heartfelt thanks every time you engage in pendulum dowsing. You may then drink the water or pour it onto a living plant such as lucky bamboo or money plant as it becomes magnetized by your spiritual vibrations.

300. Choose or Make a Pendulum

Through history, pendulums have been used to find water, precious metals, gems, oil, and gas as well as lost people, lost objects, ghosts, and negative earth energies. While a common type of pendulum is a forked stick, other types are made of a piece of string, cord, or chain with some kind of weight hanging from one end. The object with weight can be made of almost anything that is not magnetized—a key, wooden bead, paperclip, a ring, metal fishing weight, quartz crystal, glass ball, or even a Chinese coin with a square hole often used in Feng Shui—that can freely swing from a lightweight cord or chain (cord length ranges from around nine to fifteen inches, whatever is most comfortable for you).

301. Suspend the Pendulum

To work with the pendulum suspend the cord with its weighted object by looping over your index finger a bit of excess cord or chain. An alternative technique is to use a bead at one end of the chain and a heavier object, say a crystal, at the other end. Place the bead between your index and middle finger of your right hand (if you are right-handed), allowing the string or chain with the crystal to dangle vertically to about an inch from the open palm of your left hand. The pendulum will swing back and forth, in circles, and/or side to side, hovering just above the open palm of your bottom hand. Picture your open palms facing each other and you will have the correct position.

302. Use the Pendulum to Determine Dates and Time

The pendulum works through the force of your intuition or sixth sense. Some people use the pendulum to find out the hour or date something will happen. For such questions, it is helpful to cut from paper a circular clock with the increments marked or use a calendar with the dates and days in squares over which you can swing the pendulum. For example, you might ask which date in August would be best to start your summer vacation. Swing the pendulum over the days you are considering and see if it gives you a sign (downward pull or wildly swinging over one of the dates).

303. Ask "Yes/No" Questions

Consider asking questions like, "Would the beginning of August be better than the end? Would the first week be better than the second? Would a weekday be better than a weekend?" And so on.

In her book, *The Art of the Pendulum*, author Cassandra Eason recommends another way to work with your pendulum and that method focuses upon a single movement—a downward pull. Ask your angel or guide to cause the pendulum to pull downward to indicate a correct choice, for example, the correct herb in a garden that would best treat what ails you.

The downward pull indicator could also be used to divine the correct piece of paper (out of several) on which you've written various options for a career move, job transition, amount to ask for in a raise. The pendulum can thus be used for clarification of information about your business ventures.

304. Protect Your Pendulum

In the process of working with the Law of Attraction, you may seek a clear and immediate response to a question. Pendulums are believed to operate as transmitters of psychic energy. They represent intuitive information expressed by your higher self or God-self through the channel of intuition. Veteran pendulum dowsers swear that the more you use the pendulum (thus relying on your intuitive powers), the more your psychic powers will develop. Your pendulum should be considered a personal sacred object or tool. You should not let others handle it and you should keep it in a velvet or silk bag when not using it.

305. Banish Self-Limiting Thoughts

Don't doubt or second guess or rationalize the answers you may receive when working with the pendulum. To do so impedes or blocks the energy from your higher Self just as surely as clutter, according to Feng Shui experts, blocks the vital energy swirling through an environment.

Working with the Law of Attraction, you know that the self-limiting thoughts and the criticisms and doubts thrown up by your inner dialogue brings upon you more of the same. When working with the pendulum, let go of doubt. Trust the truth of the information you receive.

306. Watch for the Number Nine

The number nine has special relevance in many magic, esoteric, and spiritual traditions. In Tarot, the ninth card of the Major Arcana is the Hermit. The image is an old man or woman who provides wisdom, guidance, training, and direction. These are beneficial when working with the Law of Attraction to manifest growth, happiness, and abundance as well as before undertaking new endeavors or to know when a karmic cycle is complete.

Pay attention when the number nine shows up in your life as it can signify that you may need to take a retreat or enter a period of isolation for your growth and renewal. Or, it might indicate that your work in a particular area or relationship is finished.

307. Locate Blocked Chakras

You have a physical body and also a subtle or spiritual body. The latter has energy pathways (nadis) and a channel (sushumna) along which lie seven major wheels or vortices of energy (chakras). Together they make up the esoteric anatomy of the subtle body. An energy imbalance or blockage in one or more of the chakras can adversely influence your spiritual work and your health and well-being. Chakra blockage or a wide open chakra in which too much energy is swirling can result in mental and physical illnesses, according to some holistic practitioners, teachers of Tantra yoga, and energy workers, such as reiki masters.

308. Align Your Chakras for Healing and Empowerment

Focusing on a particular chakra as part of your regular spiritual work yields gifts of empowerment as the chosen chakra becomes more energized. When chakra energy becomes imbalanced and is too strong or diminished, illnesses in the physical body can develop.

When you feel as if your vibration no longer rises into higher (or deeper) realms of consciousness, you may need a little chakra tune up. To obtain optimum results in your work with the Law of Attraction, you want your mind, body, and spirit to be in harmonious alignment and the chakras functioning as intended. For those times, when they aren't, there are many excellent ways to heal chakra issues—reiki or touch therapy, crystals and gem work, and aura cleansing, to name a few.

309. Create a Chakra Chart

The Muladhara, or root chakra, represents the site of your spiritual potential. Swadhisthana is the center of unconscious desire while Manipura is associated with your spiritual forcefulness or dynamism. Love emanates from the Anahata chakra. The Vishuddha represents the site of wisdom and the ability to discern between truth and ignorance. The Ajna chakra is associated with sacred prayer while Saharara is the center of higher consciousness.

You can create a chakra chart by drawing a large circle on paper with seven circles ringing the internal perimeter. Allowing the pendulum to swing over each of the seven circles symbolizing the chakras, ask your "yes/no" questions about chakra blockages, spiritually based physical illness, and appropriate healing methodologies.

310. Refocus Your Vision During Transitions

Patterns of thinking can radically shift when you are in any of the big transitions of life such as having a baby, making a major purchase, grieving over the loss of a loved one, moving to another state away from your support network and family, suffering a major illness, or renovating a house when you literally experience the breaking down of old structures. Thought patterns can become fearful, anxious, and doubtful, dragging down your emotional energy. Those times would be good periods to work with the pendulum to re-energize your vision, intent, and goal. Use your pendulum to get answers and information about the most pressing issues or insight into what life lesson you are in the throes of learning.

311. Strengthen Self-Care and Turn Love upon Yourself

One of the most vital aspects of working with the Law of Attraction requires that you take care of yourself. Self care begins with self nourishment and self acceptance. Only when you have these things will you find meaning in all the other things you desire to attract. The love of your life can show up but if you aren't emotionally healthy enough to receive him or her, the relationship won't satisfy for long.

Love yourself as though you were showing love to your spouse or lover. When you are in love, you have energy to spare. You are happy, perhaps obsessively so as you consider doing special things for that special someone. Do those things for you.

312. Get Up and Connect with Life

You can use the pendulum dousing techniques you've learned in this chapter to help you understand how to treat yourself better. You may not feel energetic enough to pick it up and start, but give yourself the opportunity to begin moving in the right direction again. If you don't move your body, it simply won't work as well. The muscles begin to shrink. Flexibility lessens along with your range of motion. You start to gain weight.

Life becomes dull. It's a snowball of things going from bad to worse. Until you shift the energy and start down a different path to becoming fully alive and engaged in your life, the Law of Attraction will continue bringing you the same old stuff.

313. Find Relief in Nature

According to Feng Shui and geomancy theories, trees, bodies of water, and living plants are all natural sources for healing energy or pranic energy. Prana is the Sanskrit word for life-sustaining or vital energy. When you feel restless and searching for answers, consider that you won't find relief and meaning in the world but rather from within the self.

Seek out a special tree, rose garden in a park, a clump of bushes in a meadow, or a gurgling stream. Draw close to such energy sources and stay near it while you ponder what ails you. Then suspend your pendulum from your fingers as previously discussed. Sit near the water or circumambulate a boulder, a mountain, a tree or bed of flowers. Attune yourself to the feelings of energy in the pendulum.

314. Access Healing Energy Through Your Pendulum

When you begin to feel tingling sensations in your fingers and arms, tiny buglike movements across your back, warm or cool energy moving along your spine, or a current coursing through your pendulum hand and arm, you can be assured that you are drawing energy from nature. Direct that energy to your heart, if it's been broken, or to whatever area in your body that most needs it. Allow healing to take place. Perhaps you are grieving and would like to ask the universe or that loved one who has crossed over a "yes/no" question. Use the pendulum. When you are finished, express your gratitude to the life-giving, fecund Goddess or divine Creator.

315. Clarify Your Dreams

Pendulum dowsing can be used to help you clarify a big dream for your life. Perhaps it's been a daydream for a long time and you have decided to work with the Law of Attraction to make it a reality. Do a mind map of your dream. Draw a big circle on a piece of paper and write your dream in the center of the circle. Then as the energy of your mind flows around the thought of your dream, began drawing spokes originating from the large circle and ending in smaller ones containing all your ideas associated with making your dream a reality. Use your pendulum and "yes/no" questions to clarify details and to help you prepare to-do lists, timelines, and goals.

Steps You Can Take . . .
to Share Your Knowledge

316. Create a Better Life by Giving of Yourself

You know people who are always complaining that they can't get ahead in life no matter what they do. They may have lost jobs, be in pain, or at risk of losing their homes. They may wonder if they are living under some kind of curse. At church, they find comfort in hearing that God loves them, watches over them, and can help them, but they don't know how to help themselves. These are people you can teach how to avail themselves of financial prosperity, joy, and success in every area of life. You can also learn from them. Questions and comments posed by others inevitably provide different lenses for examining a subject. Sharing knowledge is often a two-way flow. Teaching someone else something is a surefire method for learning more about it yourself.

317. Teach Others to Fish

The Taoist Lao Tzu once expounded that if you give a man a fish, he eats for a day but if you teach him to fish he can then eat for the rest of his life. The point is not to promote another person's reliance upon you to keep providing the fish, but to empower that individual to find his own sustenance from life. When he understands how to manifest in alliance with the Law of Attraction his heart's many desires and his body's assorted needs, he will be able to sustain himself without your intervention. That is not to say you can't emotionally and psychologically support him and others.

318. Remember That There's Enough for Everyone

A common question that pops up in conversations about the Law of Attraction is that if everyone gets to have as much abundance in their lives as they want, won't that take something away from others? The answer is no. The world of formless energy and substance out of which all of creation takes shape is boundless and limitless. It's not a scale that tips when weight is added or rises when something is removed. Perceiving the truth that an abundant life is available for all may require a new way of thinking for some people.

319. See Beyond Limits

Enlightened beings from ancient times to the present day have said that the creation of the universe (or multiverse for those who believe that there could be infinite universes), occurred first in the Divine Mind where ideas of less and lack and their opposites do not exist. The infinite Divine Mind perceives everything in perfection and completeness, beyond duality, ever present and without the limitations of time, space, and dimensions.

Even if everyone on earth understood how to manifest a pink Cadillac and everyone received a car, the infinite storehouse of the universe could still provide a car for everyone who wanted two or three or more. You can have as many as you want. It simply requires your thinking consecutive thought that is sustained over time.

320. Don't Judge by Appearances

Appearances of things (for example, disease) can produce that idea in the mind and it will manifest in the body. But if you know the truth, for example, that disease is not the true reality—health is— then you can let go of the appearance and embrace the truth. This is an important concept for those wanting financial prosperity (who see the absence of wealth and consider poverty as truth).

When a person's faith is strong enough to see the body's illness as no more than an illusion or spiritual error in the mind, that faith restores perfection and wholeness. This is another important truth to be shared with others desiring to work with the Law of Attraction to attract optimum health.

321. Empower Others Everywhere You Go

Do as the late author Alex Haley (*Roots*) advocated, "Find the good and praise it." Celebrate life and let your enthusiasm for doing good and seeing good be a lightning rod for others that they will desire to live in that kind of happiness. Remind yourself and others that in every moment is the power to change the course of your day or your life. You can encourage others to recognize the negatives in their thoughts and behaviors. Since they alone own them, they must be the ones who shift the paradigm. By choosing to break the destructive cycles of negative thoughts, words, and actions and to move into alignment with positive and happy thinking, feeling, doing, and speaking, they become empowered to move beyond the appearances of limitations.

322. Join a Networking Group

Not surprisingly, many people working with deliberate intention and the Law of Attraction have sought and found support among others who share their ideas about how to achieve the good things in life such as wealth and abundance. Sometimes members of a Law of Attraction networking group will help you clarify and establish goals or work toward new ones and you, in turn, help them stay on track. The group can help you identify behaviors that may create luck to bring success or factors that may be chasing it away. You reinforce each other's pursuit of goodness, not just the acquisition of material wealth but in the expectation that your sacred dreams, goals of working service groups, and humanitarian efforts to help individuals and communities in the world will find fruition.

323. Set a Shining Example

People who are successful in creating their exciting dream life are always on the move. They don't sit still and wait for life to come to them. They won't write one book in a year, they'll write two, four, or five. They won't start just one business in a lifetime. They will build one until it becomes mega successful, and then they'll begin again with something new. They sail into life each day with zeal and gusto, ever on the lookout for a new idea, a more fun way to do something, a new enterprise, ever challenging the status quo. By demonstrating that passionate way of being, you are demonstrating how to best work with the law. You may be motivating yourself as well.

324. Learn about Metaphysical and Esoteric Teachings

Some Law of Attraction proponents join support groups to share metaphysical or esoteric teachings behind the Law of Attraction. Others like the open and honest ways that members engage in self-disclosure and friendship. They no longer feel isolated in the pursuit of a new and better life. Still others find that it helps to work with fellow Buddhists or survivors of some life-threatening disease who support one another through several layers of common interest such as a desire for compassionate living or a sense of shared common ground.

325. Show Others How to Create a New Life

Some Law of Attraction teachers talk about how to get everything you want from positive thinking. They expound various points they believe key to becoming an attraction magnet for abundance of every kind. Many people will remain skeptical and won't believe that it is possible to create such a life until they see someone else do it. Show them how to create a good life, centered in thanksgiving and gratitude. Inspire others to become self-reliant and independent.

It is helpful when sharing with others information critical to working with the law to emphasize that the most successful individuals refuse to settle for mediocrity in life. They see change as exciting and necessary. In fact, they create it when forming intention for their new life of prosperity and joy.

326. Emphasize Persistence

Another key point to emphasize is the importance of persistence, not only formulating the belief that a goal is worthwhile but continuing to believe that the goal can be reached. Further, it is critical that an individual who is starting to work with the law firmly believes that he is worthy of the goals and desires he sets forth to achieve. He must have the persistence of Henry Ford, whose engineers at first did not believe it was possible to create a six-cylinder motor, and hold on passionately to his vision despite the naysayers.

327. Offer Help to a Younger Generation

Young people today face many of the same challenges of growing up as those of previous generations but, in addition, must find ways to deal with media messages that glorify negative patterns of thinking and living. Teachers, youth counselors, parents, and peers could do more to help the younger generation see others as themselves, to celebrate the success of others as if it were their own, to promote the interests of others as if they were self-serving interests. It's a radical concept to teach young people but if they can conceive that all of humanity is interconnected on some level and that one act of goodness affects everyone, perhaps they would be inspired to living noble lives.

328. Teach Teens to Teach Others

Many teens, as they push up against the boundaries of their world as part of their biological task to individuate away from the family, sometimes tune out adult guidance. But they listen to each other. One of the best ways to get across a message of hope is to let the teens spread it among themselves. Remind them that it is possible to change the world one person at a time and that making the world a better place for everyone, including future generations, is an admirable goal. Just imagine how such teaching might help someone scared and confused and ready to give up completely on his or her life.

329. Take the Law of Attraction into Schools

Surely it could greatly benefit young people to learn about how they can create a positive and meaningful life for themselves. A self-centered, decadent lifestyle that leaves you burned out by the age of thirty does not benefit the individual, the family, the community, or society at large. Begin to reach out to young people to give them the tools to go after their dreams. Offer to participate in career day at your local high school. Use that venue to discuss how the Law of Attraction helped you find the right job, get promoted, start your own company, or furthered your career. Show genuine passion and enthusiasm for your work and your life to inspire your young audience. Use concrete examples from your life.

330. Offer Your Wisdom through Community Outreach

Why not put together a proposal for a workshop on the Law of Attraction (based on your personal results, shared stories from others, and in-depth knowledge) through an adult education program sponsored by your local park and recreation center. If you can't write a book, record your ideas in booklet form. Offer to sell it for a $1.00 as part of your seminar or presentation. You will be sharing the information and creating a small income stream that could possibly grow into a home-based business.

331. Reach Out to Those in Their Golden Years

Senior citizens represent a sector of the population who could use knowledge of the Law of Attraction. They are often vulnerable, sometimes suffering more than others from a lack of money, health-care coverage, affordable medications, and sometimes even food and housing. Sharing techniques and strategies for intentionally working with the Law of Attraction might help members of the aging population create not only longer and healthier lives but a better quality of the life they have left. While they may not have the energy of their youth or the same dreams, nevertheless, some may still hope to find a pot of gold at the end of the rainbow and likely would share it with others.

332. Include Gratitude in Your Teaching

Through the sharing of your experience with others of intentionally working with the Law of Attraction, remember to include a discussion of the roles of faith and gratitude.

Teaching others about the law so that they might have better lives, happiness, and a more prosperous future has resonance in the Buddhist idea of humanity's interconnectedness and the necessity of each person having a sense of responsibility toward the welfare of others. In Buddhism, the highest ideal is the path of the bodhisattva. The bodhisattva finds the source of all fulfillment, that is the Ultimate Truth, but he denies himself enlightenment in order to bring all other fellow beings to that same holy Source.

Steps You Can Take . . .

to Transform Your Life

333. Ask Yourself: What's Next?

You can now draw to yourself a brighter future, vibrant health, transformational thinking, financial prosperity, abundance of every kind, and deeper and more profound spiritual connections. You have risen above the fetters that have been holding you back through self-limiting thought to discover the world anew. You have allowed your newfound sense wonder to inspire feelings of gratitude. But what if, after you have attracted to you everything you ever dreamed of, emotion still tugs at your heart. Perhaps it's your sense of altruism asking you to give as generously as you've received.

334. Think about Who Else You Can Help

As you previously learned, you can't change another human being, but you can choose to behave differently around that person and that is enough to shift the dynamics of a relationship with him or her. If you are in a bad relationship, dissatisfied with your employer, or have reached the end of your patience with a disgruntled client, you can choose to end the connection and go in a different direction in your life. Bless those individuals as you move forward. But why not also see them bathed in holy light in your mind and silently bless them that they may have the highest good that can come to them? Ask yourself, "Who else might benefit from my knowledge of how to work with the Law of Attraction?"

335. Keep an Eye Out for Opening Doors

Perhaps one of the most important things the late mythologist Joseph Campbell said that resonated with American psyches was to follow your bliss. Maybe a door has closed on your marriage or career. Perhaps now the time is right to visit Italy or France, even buy a villa or farmhouse, set up your software business in Ireland, start your import store on E-Bay, establish an orphanage in India, a school in Nepal, or a hospital in Africa. If those ideas seem too grand, consider doing some volunteer work at home or abroad. Use the Law of Attraction to draw in those doors that Campbell said will open as you follow your bliss. As they do swing open, confidently walk through them. Just as the law has drawn a door closed, it will open others and help you across the threshold.

336. Keep a Light Heart

Are you someone who laughs easily at the craziness of life? Or do you take every thing seriously? You have already learned how important emotion is in magnetizing thought. Find the inner child and laugh often with his or her childhood delight as you move into your new life of working with the Law of Attraction. You'll find humor helps defuse tense situations, adds levity to the most serious moments, and ensures that you never take yourself (or anyone else, for that matter) too seriously.

337. Use the Law for Material or Spiritual Gain

The Law of Attraction is available to all. But some practice working with it more than others. You might choose to make an in-depth study of its working in your life and the lives of others. From your work and special expertise and insights, you could charge fees that could become an income stream, perhaps the means of helping yourself get out of debt or begin to build wealth. Doing such work with a sense of high-minded purpose, and not greed, makes it noble. However, you might also decide that you want to help others less fortunate and pursue Law of Attraction work as a purely spiritual endeavor. When you are motivated by selflessness to do good for others, your activities generate spiritual dividends.

338. Create a Collective Vision for Global Change

Consider how you join in with others working with the Law of Attraction to build a better world. With them, you would need to be unified in purpose, hold the same collective vision and intentions, and make a deep emotional commitment to imagine a world without war, leaders coming up with solutions to global social ills, and corporations becoming good citizens and even responsible stewards of the planet. Perhaps you and your group could focus on the eradication of hunger, cures for HIV/AIDS and cancer, abolition of racism and bigotry, and other issues.

339. Recognize that You are a Part of the Planet

Think of yourself as one member of a global family who works with the Law of Attraction to envision well-being of planet Earth. Many people, not just those embracing the Gaia philosophy, are persuaded that much has to be done to reduce the human footprint, not only on Earth but in the heavens.

As you begin to manifest helpful people, wonderful relationships, the things you've always wanted, begin to think "outside the box" in radical new ways. Try envisioning new life goals, determining a new purpose or career path, or projecting new plans for a business or organization.

340. Work to Bring about Ecological and Environmental Change

You can join with others to dream a grand dream of ecological and environmental change. Develop affirmations for group recitation. Prepare and implement to-do or action lists that might include calling upon government representatives to ensure environmentally friendly products, good alternatives to fossil fuels, safer food supplies through reduction of harmful pesticides and hormone injections of animals to increase body size, responsible e-waste recycling, preservation of the rain forests, and safer water supplies.

341. Exercise Mind and Body Control for Perfect Health

By using the Law of Attraction, you can manifest perfect mental and physical health. Using the power of your mind you can bring about healthy changes in your body, even overcome the kinds of diseases that can shorten your life. Life extension is certainly possible through an understanding of dietary rules, thoughtful consideration of eating, exercising, stress reduction, smoking cessation, and moderate consumption of coffee and alcohol, and deliberate work to manifest perfect health in harmony with the Law of Attraction.

You can learn to increase your vitality by becoming like a yogi, yoking your will to the energy you already have and using the Law of Attraction to draw more energy in from the Cosmic Source. Avoid declaring that you are tired for doing so makes you instantly feel depleted. Instead, affirm that all the energy you need is flowing into your body now.

342. Do as the Yogis Do

Some Indian yogis have been able to slow their heartbeat and breathing in order to demonstrate mental power over their bodies. Satya Sai Baba, a controversial Hindu holy man born in the Indian village of Puttaparthi, can manifest things out of the air by the power of his thought. He has done hundreds of demonstrations throughout his lifetime and is considered by millions to be an avatar or incarnation of God. When he materializes things such as gems and sacred ash, he is said to chant, "It is coming now." That phrase, spoken with resolve and faith implicit in it, is an excellent one to use when working with the Law of Attraction.

343. Access Altered States of Consciousness

You may not have yet reached such transcendental states of consciousness as to be able to know your past and future, but perhaps using the Law of Attraction you can draw that ability, know how to use it, and experience fantastic results. Some esoteric teachers say it is the destiny of each person to evolve spiritually. If you need a teacher to guide you, you can attract him or her into your life and anything else you need. Whatever you can think of with feeling again and again, you can make it so.

Saints of various cultures have been able to know, see, or do things that seem beyond human ability. The Sufi mystics known as the dervishes dance themselves into altered states of consciousness. Shamans of certain cultures also perform sacred dance to bring about trance. They have shown transcendence over the body that defies a logical and rational understanding of how the human organism functions. Undoubtedly, they have been able to tap into something far greater and more powerful than simple human intellect and emotion. They have set up an attraction for spiritual awakening and the transcendental states of consciousness become the doorway between ordinary consciousness and the transcendent mind.

344. Awaken Your Powerful Energy Centers

Your body contains two extremely powerful energy centers, the heart and the crown chakras. Your destiny, and that of everyone, some say, is to be transformed into spiritually evolved beings. That happens through the awakening and ascent of the kundalini energy up through the spinal channel known as the sushumna. Kundalini is the divine transformational energy that activated or awakened can bestow knowledge of the past and future, the mysteries of the universe, the secrets of all creation.

The Law of Attraction will bring you what you deeply desire and need—if that is a teacher to help you on your spiritual path, you have only to ask for him or her. There's an old adage that states that when the student is ready, the teacher appears.

Your greatest benefit of an awakened kundalini is the culmination of the process of spiritual maturation. Kundalini arousal can bring about self-realization or the recognition of the atman, knowledge of the true self. Some say it confers immortality.

345. Trigger the Awakening of Divine Energy

Some yogis and yoginis say that you can attract the conditions for the awakening of the kundalini through mantra, mudra, breath work, meditation, and other spiritual practices. The kundalini awakening can occur spontaneously or through shaktipat, the transference of energy from a teacher to his student for the purpose of initiation and awakening of the kundalini. Such awakening confers powers from all the energy centers of the body and brings about super consciousness.

You may feel pressure, especially at the base of the spine, a column of heat from the tailbone to the top of the head, sounds such as tinkling bells or thunder, sensation of ants crawling along the spine, the sound of the cosmic vibration of atoms heard as AUM, and cool and hot energy flowing along the spinal column. These are just some of the signs and symptoms. Others have heard bees buzzing, and seen (through the third eye chakra) streams of light. In India, some practitioners of yoga have found themselves spontaneously doing certain yoga poses or mudras (hand positions).

346. Live in the Eternal Now

Kundalini Shakti is perceived as a manifestation of the energetic feminine form of the Divine. When you decide to seek a higher spiritual life and begin to attract wisdom and spiritual understanding instead of "stuff," she will begin to open and empower the energy centers of the body, according to the teachings of Kundalini Maha yoga. You will become transformed. Instead of living in a material world and having your body senses dictating how you live your life, you can choose to live out your days in a different way, that is, from the inside out.

When your heart is open and your mind is beyond duality thinking, you can truly live in the present moment with consciousness of all moments—past, present, and future—contained in one time/space continuum. Yogis say that for such holy beings, there is nothing that can't be known or done.

347. Develop the Latent Powers Within You

The purpose of life, some believe, is self-development and the unfolding of the divine latent powers within. Dr. Deepak Chopra, in his book *The Seven Spiritual Laws of Success,* references the Law of Pure Potentiality, also known as the Law of Unity (because underlying infinite diversity is the unity of the One). These are universal laws just as is the Law of Attraction. As you dream this dream of your life, you are tapping into the realm of infinite possibility. It isn't to be found outside of you but rather within.

The Law of Karma will bring experiences into your life as you consciously and unconsciously send out your thoughts, but you get to decide how to handle what comes. Imagine the possibilities of always knowing the right thing to do and the right moment in which to do it. Consider being able to block illness from ever coming into your body or attract unfathomable wealth. Imagine being able to traverse the cosmos by imagery and thought. Think about how you might use infinite power and wisdom for peace and high and noble purposes. You have the power to transform yourself into self-realized or enlightened being.

348. Switch on Enlightenment

When you desire enlightenment, the power switch is flipped on, light dispels darkness or ignorance. Your usual state of being becomes one of peace and joy (or bliss). Enlightened, you possess the kingdom of God, for in the state of self-realization, you become godlike. According to some yogis, God-realized individuals know all that is knowable and even if the sacred texts from all religious paths were destroyed, a god-realized being could re-create them. People won't recognize you by all the "stuff" you have attracted and manifested but rather by your expression of love, wisdom, and power. Find the secret hidden deep inside your heart. As Rumi, the Sufi mystic might say, someone is calling you . . . maybe it's your own soul asking you to open the door.

CHAPTER 20

Steps You Can Take . . .
to Get Started Right Now

349. Set Your Intentions

You know what you want, but if you were asked to describe that item in detail, could you do it? The universe will bring you exactly what you ask for so it is important that you be specific. Often when you see something you want, you will perhaps remember only the general shape, maybe the color, and perhaps a detail or two. Establish a clear statement of your intention for manifesting a particular object with as many details as possible.

First, name the category of the material thing you most desire to manifest (for example, car, house, boat, jewelry, furniture, art, musical instrument, dishware, clothing, electronic item, or something else).

Then, name the specific item/make or style (for example, a car might be a Mercedes S-500; a musical instrument might be a Gibson folk guitar or a Stradivarius violin; an electronic item might be a Toshiba Satellite Pro laptop or seventy-five-inch plasma LCD screen).

350. Employ All Your Senses

What does the object of your desire taste like? Of course, this may not be relevant to the object you desire to manifest, but if it happens to be one hundred-year-old bottle of Scotch, being able to imagine the taste will be important. Does it have a scent? Is so, write down your thoughts about what it smells like (new clothes or wooden instruments may have subtle scents, for example, while a piece of china probably will not have a scent). What does it sound like? Sound may not have relevance for some objects but for cars, musical instruments, computers or electronic equipment, the sound it makes is an important detail. Mentally run your fingers over the object of your desire. How does it feel? What is its texture (for example, smooth and sensuous, rugged and rough, or something else)?

351. Write Down Your Declaration of Intention

Now that you have employed your senses of sight, taste, touch, scent, and sound in order to better imagine the object you intend to manifest, write a simple declaration of your intention here. Here is an example to get you started.

I am elated to know that the Law of Attraction is in the process of bringing into my life the (name of the object) that I deeply desire. I can see it clearly in my mind now (mentally imagine it) and am grateful (feel the gratitude) that it already exists in the realm of pure potentiality. I deserve this, am ready to receive it, and know that it is on its way to me and in the right moment it will manifest in my life.

352. Refine Your Declaration Language

Use breath work or meditation to move into a quiet, centered place in your mind where you can name and visualize the object, experience, or relationship that you desire to manifest. Tell the universe what it is you want. Notice if you used any negative words in your statement. For example, "I don't want any more bills." Check in with your feelings. How does the word "bills" make you feel? Most likely, it makes you feel negative. Rephrase your statement to couch it in positive terms and get rid of words like "don't," "won't," and "can't." Replace the negative statement with a positive one such as, "I desire financial prosperity and the means to easily meet my financial responsibilities." Now how do you feel? Notice the difference.

353. Fix Visualization Problems

The mind/body connection ensures that you will experience feelings in response to your mental visualization. Let's say you need to attract powerful and influential people into your career path. Consider the imagery you are using to depict them in your mind. If you see powerful people as stern, harsh, and demanding and bringing into your life more misery, stress, and unreasonable deadlines and responsibilities, you most likely will feel apprehension and dread. Instead, re-imagine them as warm, friendly, helpful, generous, and wise associates, perhaps even mentors with vested interest in you advancing in your chosen field of endeavor.

354. Eliminate Images that Cloud Your Vision

Perhaps you dream of having a trim, flexible, and muscular body, but can't get rid of the extra pounds gained during your pregnancy. You started a walking program with neighborhood friends and are now eating a healthy, balanced diet and still the weight clings. In your mind, you see yourself in the bikini you wore at eighteen and you are doing affirmations. Why isn't it working? The problem is that deep down on a subconscious level, you know you can never be eighteen with that same body again.

355. Create a New Image

Try taking a picture of yourself as you look today. Adjust your body size using scissors or a computer tool such as Photoshop. You want to create an image that your mind believes is possible to achieve. Psychological experts say that any time there is a struggle between the conscious and unconscious mind, the unconscious wins. You must convince yourself that a flexible and leaner body is possible for the person you are now. Start with a photo image, make it plausible. Paste that image on your refrigerator, bathroom mirror, and scales. Feel gratitude for each pound or inch lost and find positive ways to reward yourself as the Law of Attraction works with you to create a beautiful, strong, healthy, and leaner body.

356. Work to Clear Blockages

Do you have a fear of success? Are you going through the steps of deliberately manifesting and yet not seeing results? Perhaps you are subconsciously blocking the outcome you seek. Cultivate positive feelings. Imagine you have just received whatever it was that you hoped to manifest. Using that moment as a point of departure into a journal entry, write about how you feel at having that object, situation, or relationship now manifested in your life. Remember that the Law of Attraction responds to feelings around specific thoughts rather than the thoughts themselves. Feel worthy. Re-direct negative self-talk into positive statements. What are some of the reasons why other people (for example, your mother, father, spouse, lover, and children) love you? Make a list of all the lovable qualities and traits you have and why you are worthy to receive the gifts from the universe that you seek. Love yourself and others the way you want to be loved and cultivate feelings of self-worth.

357. Make Every Day the Best Day of Your Life

If something goes wrong in your day, shift the energy of that moment as soon as possible. Don't go through an entire day with a negative attitude after breaking the handle off a china cup at the kitchen sink because you awoke late for an important early morning meeting. Listen to beautiful music, get physical and take walk, lie down for a quick power nap, rejuvenate and refresh by doing some yoga or breath work, listen to a Law of Attraction tape or CD, or offer a prayer of thanks to the Divine. You have a phenomenal power in every moment of your life to change that moment, to shift the negatives into neutral or positive energy, and to regain forward impetus.

358. Focus On What You Want

Perhaps you can easily recount all the reasons why you don't own your own home and perhaps paramount among those reasons are lack of savings and income. But you deeply desire to own a house to call your own. Make a list of all the positive reasons why you deserve it, how living there will change your life and the lives of your spouse, children, and pets. As a point of departure for writing about your hopes and dreams and feelings of love and gratitude, imagine a celebratory meal with relatives, a holiday gathering, or a quiet peaceful moment in your own home. Take a mental snapshot of how you feel after that writing exercise. Remember those positive feelings every time you move into feelings of lack.

359. Fine-Tune the Direction of Your Desires

Be decisive when working with the law. Remember it is always at work to bring you the things you mentally focus on, both positive and negative. Think of your mind as a canoe floating along the river of life. Buffeted and buoyed by forces of energy (wind and currents) that you can't see. For certain, that canoe is going somewhere, perhaps places you like or don't. Instead of going with the flow, remember that you have power to navigate the direction you desire to go through the paddles of your feelings and thoughts.

360. Create Space in Your Life What You Desire to Manifest

Consider that the new love of your life might not come in until your current relationship has ended. If there is a lot of negative emotional baggage associated with the relationship you are in, you have to clear out those patterns of thought and replace them with positive feelings of anticipatory excitement, hope, expectation that your clear and determined focus is attracting to you the new love you desire and deserve.

361. Create a Vacuum for Manifesting

Release what isn't working in your life and open your heart and mind to allow in new energy, relationships, and surprises that the universe may be ready to give you.

Shift the status quo when the passion dies. If you hate your job and want to find a new one or even start your own business, tender your resignation. Bless and release the old work and get started manifesting your dream vocation. Feel the excitement of embarking upon a new path to a new dream. Brainstorm, write a business plan, figure out marketing, find funding, and set your dream into forward motion. When you do, you'll see how the universe puts the wind into the sail of your ship and pushes you quickly onto your chosen course.

362. Clear the Clutter from Your Life

Energy flow is impeded when you are surrounded by clutter. Get that energy moving again by removing things that you no longer use, don't work properly, or are broken. Also put away pictures and the myriad things throughout your house that remind you of the demise of relatives and friends. Establish a special designated area in your home to honor them (for placement, read books about Feng Shui). Nourish relationships with helpful people and you'll open yourself to the inflow of healing, vibrant, and beneficial energy.

363. Reprogram Your Thoughts

Your outer life is a manifestation of your inner thoughts and feelings. When you release old patterns of negative thinking and replace them with powerful positive thoughts and expectations that make you feel hopeful and happy, you thrust into forward motion vibrations that can then attract an abundance of good things to you. Do you desire love with a man who is trustworthy, capable, and emotionally healthy? Examine your thoughts to see why he is not already in your life. Maybe the pain and drama associated with a previous relationship caused you to fear a future one. But if you can't imagine the possibility of a wonderful new love, how will it ever come to you?

364. Use Your Dreams

Place a pad of paper and a pencil next to your bed, or even better, purchase and use a dream journal (any blank book will due). Upon awakening, remain in that sleepy state and notice how you feel from having that dream. Try to recall all the images you can about your dream. Without judging or analyzing your dream, write everything you can remember about the dream, especially your feeling and mood as you awakened. After you have recorded your dream, consult a good dream dictionary to choose meanings for the symbols that make sense to you. Once you have interpreted all the symbols, action, messages, theme, and any particularly potent images, rewrite the dream to expose its relevance and meaning; meaning can be revealed in the layers of the dream or even over a period of time during which you dream that same dream. Consult books about dream work to learn how to extract as much meaning as possible.

365. **Trust Yourself**

Learn to rely on your emotional guidance system of intuition or sixth sense to know when to let go. If something is not right in your life, you may be overriding the signals from your emotional guidance system that warn you to steer clear or break away. The more you rely on your inner guidance, the more you will trust it when it warns you to shift direction. Sometimes just a little shift is all that is need to create a vacuum for financial prosperity and abundance that you may seek.

Index
